C000023405

WALKING
is
TRANSPORT

Mayer Hillman
Anne Whalley

Vol. XLV No. 583

© Policy Studies Institute 1979.
All rights are reserved. No part of this publication may be reproduced, stored in a retrieval system, or transmitted, in any form or by any means, electronic, electrical, chemical, mechanical, optical, photocopying, recording or otherwise, without the prior permission of the copyright owner.

ISBN 0 85374 173 5

Published by Policy Studies Institute, 1-2 Castle Lane, London SW1E 6DR
Printed by Dawson & Goodall Ltd., The Mendip Press, Bath

Contents

List of Tables and Figures

Introduction

It is a well known fact, though usually unquantified, that nearly all personal travel involves walking, either as the sole means of travel on a journey or as one or more of its stages. However, there has been scant research on the subject of pedestrian travel and, as a result, little is known about its characteristics or about the changes that have occurred over time. Thus it is not surprising that walking has been poorly represented in transport policy, and that the consequences for those in society whose travel needs are frequently met on foot are not brought to light. It was with the intention of contributing to a remedy for this situation that the Trustees of the Rees Jeffreys Road Fund decided to support this research project.

Previous studies of personal mobility and accessibility at Political and Economic Planning (PEP)[1] suggested that walking has perhaps been neglected and given too low a priority in transport policy and practice. Symptomatic of the neglect, it was suggested, had been the dearth of comprehensive data on pedestrian travel which could be used for detailed study.

One step was taken to make good this omission in 1972/73 when the Department of the Environment carried out a large scale national survey into the travel habits of the population, part of which included a comprehensive record of all journeys made—on foot as well as by other methods. However, the published findings, first available in 1975, excluded all journeys on foot which were under one mile in length. A second, almost identical National Travel Survey (NTS) was carried out during 1975/76 under the control of the Department of Transport, and by the time our research was begun it was possible for outside customers to commission tables from this department, from the 'raw data' of both surveys. The authors of this book thus took the opportunity to analyse the almost untouched data on walk journeys of all lengths in the two surveys, relating them to general information about the respondents, their households, and the areas in which they lived.

---

[1] Mayer Hillman, Irwin Henderson and Anne Whalley, *Personal Mobility and Transport Policy,* PEP Broadsheet No. 542, (1973), and *Transport Realities and Planning Policy,* PEP Broadsheet No. 567, (1976); and Mayer Hillman and Anne Whalley, *Fair Play for All: a study of access for sport and informal recreation,* PEP Broadsheet No. 571, (1977).

1

The information about journeys was obtained from the travel diaries kept by each respondent over the period of a week. On the first six days they recorded details of all mechanised journeys and of walk journeys if they were at least one mile long; on the final day of the survey they recorded details of all journeys, irrespective of distance, and thus it is this 'seventh day' record which contains the full picture of pedestrian travel.[2] Diaries were completed at all times of the year and the 'seventh day' fell on different days of the week for different respondents. The picture which emerges is therefore equivalent to a film taken over a whole year with 70 to 80 different actors taking part on each of the 365 days. The surveys are described in more detail in Appendix A of this book.

The research takes a strategic view of walking. Like the car or public transport, walking features as a major component in travel activity, as it is used as a method of travel for getting to the whole range of destinations needed for the purposes of day-to-day life. The study therefore is concerned with walking primarily in the context of journeys made wholly on foot. It does not aim to examine the 'nitty-gritty' of walking—design considerations, such as kerb heights, gradients, and pavement widths—nor the unique problems of blind and disabled people. Neither is it concerned with walking as a leisure activity, though journeys on foot whose prime purpose was recreational were included in the NTS unless they were solely within the confines of a formal park. And the study does not analyse the pattern of journeys of which just a small part was on foot—from home to bus stop or from parking meter to office. Nevertheless, the remaining element of walking is far from insubstantial, representing well over one third of all the journeys made by the population at large.

The book has ten chapters. The first reviews the consideration given to walking in past policy, practice and research. The next two chapters indicate the extent of walking as an element of total travel and in the lives of different people; they also document the vulnerability of pedestrians as shown by road accident statistics. Chapter IV investigates some planning factors of significance in understanding the pattern of daily travel. Chapters V to IX examine the importance of walking in relation to five broad categories of journey—journeys to school, work and shops, visits to other essential places (such as clinics, and post offices), and travel to social and leisure activities. Chapters II to IX are based mainly on data from both of the National Travel Surveys, and as well as analysing the broad pattern of pedestrian travel they also discuss the change in travel which is indicated by the difference between the two sets of survey results. They include, too, information and data from other sources, for instance about changes in the provision and planning of facilities which could influence travel on foot. The final chapter summarises the main findings of the study, draws conclusions from them and then discusses the implications for transport policy.

---

[2] In fact, in 1975/76 the 'seventh-day' record excluded journeys on foot of less than 50 yards.

It is hoped that the research will contribute to a broad understanding of the characteristics of pedestrian travel and of the processes involved in it. It should thereby be of practical value to decision makers and practitioners in the field of transport planning, as well as being of interest to the general population—all 55 million or so of whom *are* pedestrians.

The authors would like to thank those officials of the Department of the Environment and Department of Transport who produced tables to their specifications from the NTS 1972/73 and NTS 1975/76—often a lengthy and detailed process. They would also like to thank the administrative staff at PSI for all the work involved in the preparation of this publication. Finally PSI is grateful to the Trustees of the Rees Jeffreys Road Fund, who provided the research grant for the study.

I Attitudes Towards Pedestrian Travel

Walking is very much a part of the reality of daily travel: it is the most universal and ubiquitous method of personal transport, and the inability to walk is seen as a major handicap in both medical and social contexts. The fact that walking is such an everyday occurrence for the great majority of the population should make it no less important to those concerned with urban planning and with transport policy and practice. But whether a brief glance is taken or lengthy examination is made of official attitudes towards walking as a method of travel, an inadequacy of attention is revealed amounting to discrimination against this 'staple diet' of the transport world.

Sources of Statistics on Travel

The development of a transport policy which would take account of people's patterns of travel could make use of the National Travel Surveys, the first of which was conducted in 1964. As noted in the introduction to this report however, it was only in one part of the 1972/73 and the 1975/76 surveys that a full record of walking was recorded. Data from the 1972/73 survey has been available since 1974, but so far no comprehensive report of its findings, incorporating pedestrian travel, has been published. This situation was criticised in 1977 in a Social Science Research Council (SSRC) Review which suggested that the delay in publishing these findings 'might be thought to be somewhat scandalous'.[1]

The only journeys on foot incorporated in the published volumes on the surveys are those of at least one mile in length, as a consequence of which the reality of daily travel is considerably distorted. For instance, as will be seen in the relevant chapters of this report, because the majority of journeys on foot are less than one mile long, nearly half the number of school journeys, over one third the number of shopping journeys, and about one third of the journeys of low income groups are lost from view, and without these journeys

---

[1]D. L. Munby, SSRC *Review of UK Statistical Sources: Road Passenger Transport, Vol III.* Nevertheless, in the transport chapter of the next volume of this series of SSRC Reviews—*Town and Country Planning*—L. F. Gebbett, the author does not even warn readers to beware of this distorting omission in drawing their attention to the published figures.

no true picture can be obtained of the balance, and changing balance, of travel.

However, the distorted figures are widely quoted, and have an apparent seal of approval since they originate from a government source. They are used by local authorities all over the country and by other bodies highly influential in the making of public policy. The true significance of journeys on foot is reduced by the use of the standard phrase employed to draw attention to the omission—'exclusive of shorter journeys on foot'—as if little of relevance to transport facts has been lost as a consequence. Not infrequently their significance is wholly overlooked by their total exclusion.

For instance, two recent publications of the Central Office of Information (COI)—*Inland Transport in Britain, 1976*, and *Town Traffic in Britain, 1977* make no reference at all to walking other than to refer to the creation of pedestrian precincts in some town centres, in spite of the fact that, as will be seen later, roughly half the journeys that are made in towns are made on foot. And in *The Next Twenty Five Years: An appraisal of the prospects and possibilities for development of the country's transportation system up to the end of the century,* the County Surveyors Society report of 1978 referred *inter alia* to the objective of 'taking into account the needs of all sections of the community' yet the report excluded walking as a transport mode. It cited a whole set of erroneous figures from the then current issue of *Transport Statistics,* such as that 66 per cent of all trips in major urban areas and 81 per cent in rural areas are made by car, whereas in reality the correct proportions are about 40 per cent and less than 60 per cent respectively.

The grounds cited for the omission of journeys on foot in the published tables, although the data on them are available, is that they were only gathered on the final day of respondents' travel diaries, and if general analysis were to be confined just to this final day, then there would be unacceptably small sample sizes for some of the other means of transport. The error of restricting the collection of walking journeys to only one of the seven days of the surveys is compounded by not incorporating even these in most of the published tables.

The format of the 1971 Census of Population tables covering the journey to work is also symptomatic of the disregard traditionally shown to walking. Although the published tables give the *numbers* of people using each travel method, the *percentage* of people who walk is omitted, while percentages are given for the other main methods including far less common ones. Thus, for instance, variations in the use of buses or bicycles in different towns are immediately apparent; variations in walking are not, though they can of course be calculated from the published figures.[2]

With this dearth of publicly available information on walking and pedestrian behaviour, it is not perhaps surprising that the official attitude in

---

[2] A further example of the lacuna can be seen in the studies accompanying the *Development of the Strategic Plan for the South East.* Whilst a table on the method of travel on the journey to work records the figures from which it can be seen that walking is far more common than bus or rail in the region, the text ignores this.

organisations concerned with transport is so dismissive and that no division within the Department of Transport and no unit within local authority transport departments have specific and overt responsibility for pedestrian travel. Plentiful evidence of these attitudes is apparent from a review of legislation, departmental Circulars, policy documents and research.

Legislation

In recent years, well after the 1959 Highways Act enabled local authorities to provide footways wherever they considered it necessary for the safety or accommodation of pedestrians, there has been a spate of legislation affecting pedestrians, some of it beneficial, some neutral, while some has been positively detrimental. For instance, the 1968 Transport Act recorded hardly any concern about the convenience of pedestrian travel, restricting itself largely to considerations of traffic, parking, and public transport.

The 1968 Town and Country Planning Act required planning authorities to institute surveys in their areas as part of the preparatory work for their development plans. These surveys were to be carried out to establish facts on the transport system and traffic but no reference was made to the need to include data on walking, although it was noted that the decline of local facilities (to which presumably most people walk) could affect traffic generation.[3] Evidence of a stronger directive to provide for pedestrians can be seen in the 1971 Town and Country Planning Act which enabled local authorities to create pedestrian precincts and to close roads to traffic so that they could be used exclusively by pedestrians. But the origin of the legislation stemmed primarily from a concern about the level of road accidents. This can be seen again in the 1974 Road Traffic Act, the clauses of which require local authorities to carry out studies into accidents in their area and to take measures to prevent them. It gave them powers to stop parking on pavements (though they have until 1980 before having to enforce the new law) and to instal road humps to control the speed of traffic. But it is made clear that such measures are to be used in the exercise of their powers for 'controlling, protecting and assisting *the movement of traffic* on the roads'.[4]

Departmental Circulars

The Department of Transport's attitude to walking as a transport mode is also reflected in the development of its policy on so-called 'pedestrianisation schemes'. A Circular in 1971[5] discussed the conversion of roads to footpaths on planning grounds (rather than solely on safety grounds as previously) and the creation of pedestrian streets, provided that the walk from the nearest bus stop is not greater than would be acceptable to elderly people or mothers with

---

[3]The subsuming of expenditure for pedestrians under the heading of highways in the terms of the 1972 Transport Supplementary Grant (TSG) system carried this relegation a stage further.
[4]Authors' italics.
[5]At the time the Department was a wing of the Department of the Environment.

young children. It is recommended that 50 metres be the limit of distance to be walked from the nearest point of vehicular penetration when a street is given over to pedestrians, though it could be noted that, when an area is given over to traffic—for instance at large scale urban intersections or on 'clearways'—there are no limits to the distance that pedestrians can be diverted.

A Circular in 1973 set out the terms under which pedestrian phases on traffic lights could be provided, even though it was admitted that this 'will inevitably introduce delay to vehicular traffic'. However, equivocation is apparent from the further statement in the Circular that these phases 'should only be provided when pedestrian problems cannot reasonably be resolved by other means, eg foot-bridges'. There was no statement to the effect that footbridges inevitably cause delay to pedestrian traffic or that they can cause hardship to people who have difficulty climbing steps because of disability or infirmity, when carrying heavy packages or when accompanying young children.

The Department's attitude to pedestrians can also be seen in the evolution of consideration given to their need to get across roads in safety. Since 1968, when pelican crossings were first introduced, successive Circulars have reflected an increasingly concessionary view. It is now accepted (a) that there are limits to the delay that pedestrians will tolerate before crossing roads, in spite of the risks entailed and therefore more flexibility is necessary in determining appropriate conditions for pedestrians to cross roads, (b) that an *average* walking speed is not an acceptable determinant of the time needed to cross a road, and (c) that the criteria for establishing the need for crossings can be waived or modified on the grounds that accidents have occurred at particular locations. A Circular in 1974 which enabled local authorities to install more pelican road crossings in view of their better safety record in reducing accidents compared with zebra crossings, contained the significant sentence that no assessment had been made of additional vehicle delay as pedestrian safety was considered the prime consideration.

On the other hand, *traffic* management is the main concern of transport planners in busy urban areas—which are often as busy with people as they are with traffic. Pedestrian crossings, islands and refuges at the centre of heavily-trafficked roads are then provided so as to accommodate the pedestrian in a system primarily oriented to maintaining traffic flows. Thus, at busy junctions, pedestrians can often make use of the red phase of traffic lights, but the 'yellow box' system which is designed to keep the actual road junction clear of stationary vehicles does not extend into the adjacent short stretches of road used by the pedestrians. Traffic is thus able to keep flowing but the pedestrian may be prevented from crossing the road by nose-to-tail traffic queueing up to the brink of the yellow box. At other junctions pedestrians are prevented from crossing a road subject to the red phase of the traffic lights because other traffic is turning into the road—'all-red' phases at light-controlled junctions are very much the exception to the rule.

The pedestrian is effectively discriminated against even in the context of crossings intended to be safe havens for them, as one in twelve pedestrian casualties occur on these crossings.[6] Moreover, additional crossings are refused if the proportion of pensioners and children using them is not sufficiently high. The installation of pedestrian phases on traffic lights on accidents grounds alone can only be justified after there have been at least five personal injury accidents[7]—preventive action is thus ruled out.

However, whilst criticism can be made of the methods employed and concern expressed about the effectiveness and resolution with which the methods have been adopted, it would be incorrect to imply that successive governments have not taken steps to reduce the number of pedestrian casualties. The measures already mentioned (pedestrian precincts and crossings) are, of course, based on the premise that there is a need to reduce the annual toll of accidents; in addition, effective use is made of the press and broadcasting media for road safety campaigns. Local authorities also employ road safety officers who, among other things, regularly visit schools in order to impress on children the need for caution.

The other government department whose activities are most relevant to pedestrian travel is the Department of the Environment (in its planning functions, formerly the Ministry of Housing and Local Government). Its policies appear to reflect better the relevance of walking to much daily activity. For instance, in its Circular on housing standards (and costs) in 1969, it advocated that accommodation designed for old people should be conveniently located within a quarter of a mile of shops, a church, bus stop, public house and post office, so that they can be reached without crossing a busy road. In this way it implied a policy of planning for people to meet their daily needs on foot. And the Department's Design Bulletin on residential roads and footpaths in 1977 set out the objective of ensuring safe and convenient pedestrian access between homes and local facilities. It suggested that pedestrians should share road space with traffic but take priority over it, this being achieved by designs which, for instance, are not compatible with vehicles travelling at 30 mph—unlike the design standards laid down in the earlier manual of 1966.

Transport Policy

The official approach to transport policy recently found expression in 1976, when the Department of the Environment published a Green Paper on the subject. The authors of the document had access to the findings of the 1972/73 National Travel Survey, but reference to these findings was selective and walking as a means of travel was ignored—in spite of repeated references to the objective of providing mobility for the large minority of the population without access to a car. Indeed, the policy approach pervading the document appeared to stem from a traffic manager's viewpoint, albeit one with a social conscience, rather than from the public's viewpoint.

---

[6]Department of Transport, *Road Accidents, Great Britain 1977*, HMSO, (1978), Table 34.

[7]This decision may be contrasted with the 85 percentile rule whereby traffic speed limits can be raised if more than 15 per cent of the traffic exceeds the limit.

However, some of the submissions made to the Secretary of State on this consultation document pointed out the significance of walking, and the subsequent 1977 White Paper, *Transport Policy,* then made many references to pedestrians: 'most of us have a stake in all transport issues. We are pedestrians'; 'for the future, therefore, we should aim to decrease our absolute dependence on transport . . . and to plan more consciously for those who walk as well as those who use mechanical transport'; 'people get to a wide range of facilities, simply by walking'. It also refers to the need for a balance between the conflicting demands of different sorts of movement—walking is included in the list—and recommends that in more ambitious schemes the needs of pedestrians should be considered from the start of planning.

Nevertheless, even this far more enlightened document does not come to terms with the special relevance that land use planning has for travel, and especially walking, nor does it consider walking adequately in all its sections, for in its discussion under the heading of 'Local Planning and Choice' in which it refers to most journeys being 'local', it goes on to describe public transport as a 'local transport need' as if it were the sole means of local travel for people without cars. And although it states that its suggested policies 'would support the national aims of energy conservation', walking is excluded from mention in the discussion of efficient travel methods and in the table of 'users' expenditure and use of resources per unit of transport'.[8]

In fact, compared with other travel methods, users' expenditure is, of course, minimal—no more than the cost of shoe-leather. Public expenditure on pedestrians is given elsewhere in the White Paper as £88 million per year: the total cost per 'passenger' kilometre, therefore, could have been calculated, using NTS data on mileage walked, as being 0.4 pence. This is about one fifth of the cost calculated in the White Paper for all motorised travel (2.2 pence). Furthermore, if the calculations were to be based on journeys, rather than miles, (because the aim of travel is to achieve journey purposes rather than miles) then the cost per journey walked turns out again to be about 0.5 pence and the cost per motorised journey to be about 25 pence. Energy costs, of course, are even more divergent.

The 1978 White Paper *Policy for Roads* expresses the government's commitment to public transport on the grounds that 'not everyone can rely exclusively (sic) on private transport' (people without a car, the elderly and those on low incomes are cited) yet walking, which is their primary travel method, is **not** even referred to. Closer reading of this White Paper confirms that the origin of this false view also stems from reliance on the published volumes of the NTS for the White Paper erroneously records that four in five of all journeys are made by car and that even in non-car owning households half the journeys are made by car, whereas in reality the proportions are nearer two in five and one

---

[8]The same omission occurs in the transport section of a recent study dealing exclusively with means of energy conservation. No reference is made to the potential of walking, in spite of detailed investigation of the potential of each area of motorised vehicle use. Gerald Leach, *et al. A Low Energy Strategy for the United Kingdom.* International Institute for Environment and Development. (1979).

in eight respectively.[9] It is clear that the authors of this White Paper also believe that distance travelled is an adequate measure of personal mobility so that the indication of a successful transport development will be that people are now travelling more than they used to.[10]

Other Government Departments

The Department of Energy can be seen also to have developed a greater awareness of the significance of walking. Its Advisory Council on Energy Conservation discussed the long-term possibilities of energy saving in its paper on transport. It referred to 'a more localised style of living' with only short trips needing to be made, a change of residence or employment to reduce the journey to work, and the dispersion of offices and factories to smaller units as three means of reducing transport demand, implying thereby that *walk*-oriented travel patterns would be more economical. The same Council, in its paper on short and medium-term considerations with regard to energy conservation in passenger transport, discussed the objective of encouraging walking (and cycling) and suggested that local authorities could be encouraged in their Transport Policies and Programmes (TTPs), and through the related Transport Supplementary Grants (TSGs), to initiate developments advantageous to pedestrians, and thereby energy-conserving.

Decisions of the Department of Education and Science also have a transport dimension insofar as local authorities have a responsibility to ensure that children not living close to their nearest school are provided with free transport. The Department has given much attention to this problem because of its obvious concern for the safety of schoolchildren and also the steeply rising cost of transport. For instance, it issued a Circular in 1965, regarding the need for greater consideration to be given to children's safety on school journeys when deciding whether or not to provide school transport. Nevertheless, the two mile limit within which children of five years and upwards have been considered able to walk has not been reduced in spite of the considerable increase in the risk they have to take in crossing roads since the limit was set in the 1940s. Apparently less thought has been given to the consequences for the safety of children travelling longer distances to the larger schools being planned—Chapter V records the extent of the change in school size in recent years. In the development of the school planning programme, the Department does not appear to have accorded much credit to the benefits of smaller schools which can be reached on foot, from the viewpoint of the convenience of the children attending them or to the cost saving in transport.

Local Authorities

In a variety of ways, local authorities are involved in the preparation and

---

[9]See Chapter III.

[10]A supreme example of this way of thinking can be seen in Richard Pryke, 'Misconceptions on Mobility' in *A Policy for Transport,* the Nuffield Foundation, (1977), pp 37-38. (Page 44 of the same document contains a rejoinder).

implementation of plans which affect the safety, convenience and access of pedestrians. Their attitudes to pedestrians are reflected in general within the context of development plans and transport plans, and in detail by the types of traffic management measures they introduce.

Broadly it can be stated that pedestrians' needs have been seen largely in terms of the conflict between the requirement to ensure safety when crossing roads and the delay to traffic that this occasions rather than in terms of convenience or access for pedestrians. As a result, pedestrian needs are catered for by traffic management measures, and the provision of subways or footbridges, zebra and pelican crossings. The measures are adequate if not always convenient, but what is perhaps questionable is the effort which goes into their application. For instance, one clause in the Road Traffic Act of 1974 requires local authorities to carry out studies into accidents and to take steps to prevent such accidents; and in the submission of their Transport Policies and Programmes, they are called upon to indicate their target for a phased reduction in accidents. Few, if any, have heeded these requests.

It was noted earlier that among pedestrians' primary concerns is the condition of pavements, for which local authorities also have responsibility. However, the increasing intrusion of street furniture and cars parked on pavements both of which pose hazards for pedestrians—particularly the poorly sighted—and the fact that in icy weather pavements are not necessarily gritted to prevent pedestrians slipping as roads are gritted to prevent vehicles skidding, suggest that the minimisation of risk of injury to pedestrians when walking on pavements does not attract the attention that the extent of travel on them seems to warrant. Some local authorities have made a contribution to accident reduction through the creation of traffic-free pedestrian zones in some new residential areas and city centres, though two cautionary notes need to be sounded about such solutions. Firstly, the risk to pedestrians outside the precincts is increased by the very fact that roads on their peripheries now carry very high volumes of traffic. Secondly, their limited applicability must be borne in mind as widespread segregation of pedestrians and wheeled traffic cannot be considered realistic in view of the insufficiency of road space in the central areas of most towns and cities, and of the high costs that such segregation would entail.

In the preparation of their development plans, few local authorities have indicated an awareness of the significance of walking as the primary method of travel of most groups in the population. The focus of attention of their transport departments has been on the resolution of problems created by the rising volumes of traffic on the roads, particularly in the rush hour. The limited capacity of the road network in their area has encouraged them to seek for improvements through road works, traffic management measures and other devices intended to accommodate more vehicles or to oblige commuters to travel by public transport in lieu of a car. Less priority has been attached to resolving what pedestrians see as being transport problems—poor accessibility and an inconvenient or unpleasant walking environment. As a result, proposals have been very much oriented towards motor traffic and the projection of its levels on the road network at various points of time in the future. The objective has typically been set down in terms of securing 'an efficient and integrated transport system which provides for maximum mobility and for a balance between public and private transport and between the road space and parking space available'. The fundamental difference between the options proposed for consideration is frequently the manner and degree to which they restrict the free flow of traffic.

Mention is rarely made of walking in Structure Plans—unless the objective of protecting and enhancing the quality of the environment can be taken to refer to it—and thus little need has been seen to gather data on the characteristics of pedestrian travel, other than occasionally in respect of rush hour travel because of its interference with traffic flow. Typically, walking is excluded from the list of 'travel methods that have their part to play in the solution of transport problems', and where it is acknowledged as a means of travel it is summarily dismissed as 'journeys on foot are generally extremely short in length and take place on minor roads'. It is also often dismissed on the grounds that it is not strategic or of 'structural importance'. (A Department of the Environment Memorandum states that issues should be of key structural importance if they are to warrant inclusion in Structure Plans,[11] though as will be seen in later chapters, far more journeys are made on foot than by public transport, and almost as many as by car).

Walking does not feature in the sections of Structure Plans devoted to specific topics: for instance, the section devoted to shopping is rarely couched in terms other than of the motorised accessibility of strategic or district centres. However recent modifications to some Structure Plans refer to the decline of mobility of those without access to a car, the benefits to be attained by reducing the need to travel through land use planning, the adoption of policies to encourage walking as an alternative to vehicular travel, the determination that roads should be used in such a way as to allow the maximum possible area for pedestrians (though with a rider that this must be consistent with parking policy), and the incorporation of walking into the modelling process. In addition local authorities contemplating applications by developers for the construction of hypermarkets or out of town shopping centres, are now advised by the Department of the Environment to give due consideration to the potential effects of such operations on the 'vitality of existing shopping centres in the wider interests of the community, including non-car owners', and to recognise the important role that corner shops and shopping parades still play in serving the needs of those within easy walking distance of them.

Many local plans, however, are still focussed on relieving traffic congestion through traffic management measures, and occasionally through increasing the capacity of the road system, rather than ensuring that people can travel conveniently on foot. More recently walking has been increasingly recognised

---

[11]Memorandum on Structure and Local Plans accompanying Department of the Environment Circular 55/77, para 2.10.

as an important means of travel which deserves to be given priority in environmental areas, and there is a greater awareness of the benefits of the local accessibility of shops and other public facilities.[12]

Transport Plans

The consultants employed to prepare Land Use Transportation Studies (LUTS) have traditionally viewed walking as an item for environmental evaluation, principally in the context of the severance effects of new roads on pedestrian movement, and for determination of the appropriate modal split for rush hour traffic when the capacity of the road system may not be adequate for unlimited car commuting. Problems of collection, definition and of memory recall among respondents have been quoted to substantiate the exclusion of data on walking from the LUTS[13], together with difficulties of 'modelling' the far greater number of journeys—the use of zones as origins and destinations for motorised, and therefore longer, journeys makes this exercise much simpler. Yet most of the major local authorities' ability to assess the effects of their policies on people's mobility and accessibility is based on this incomplete information gathered in the surveys forming part of the LUTS.

Moreover, after being used in LUTS, the information may continue to be used in the determination of subsequent policies. For instance, the transport policies for London, as set out in the current *Transport Policies and Programmes* of the Greater London Council for the period 1979-84 rely on the limited data gathered in the London Traffic Survey of 1962 and the Greater London Transportation Survey of 1971. In the circumstances, it is not surprising that neither within 'the four main elements of its strategy for transport' nor as one of 'the major features and aims of transportation policy', within the general strategy, does walking warrant a mention—in spite of the aim of the strategy being to 'meet Londoners' demands for mobility'. The needs of pedestrians are in fact discussed in a few lines in the section on traffic management and parking control immediately after the Council's policy is stated to be 'to make the most efficient use of the existing road system, to give priority to traffic essential to London's economy'. The Department of the Environment Circular 104/73 which calls on local authorities in their Transport Policies and Programmes (TPPs) in include proposals covering expenditure in the whole transport field—including pedestrians—is clearly not seen by some authorities to require a significant modification in their thinking.

Dependence on survey data, the inadequacy of which reflects the same blinkered attitude towards pedestrian travel, recurs in London Transport plans for the future: in its forecasting exercise 'prepared as an input to the 5-year plan', walking is again excluded so that, for instance, two-thirds of trips of pensioners in London are said to be made by public transport—but if walking

---

[12]See for instance, *A Plan for Camden:* London Borough of Camden's District Plan Written Statement, 1977, Section 4.

[13]See page 5 for reasons given for exclusion of data on walking from the published volumes of the NTS.

were included, the true proportion would be less than one third. The need to incorporate data on walking in the forecasting exercise is apparent from the fact that choice of travel mode is far more likely to be made between walking and public transport than between car and public transport.

However, several of the post-1973 LUTS reflect a better appreciation of the variations in personal mobility among different groups in the population. Some studies have collected more comprehensive survey data on walking in order to assess catchment areas of facilities (such as schools and shops), and to analyse the effect of traffic management measures, such as the creation of environmental areas (through which no through-traffic is allowed but out of which pedestrians have to cross a more traffic-dominated circumferential road system).[14]

In recognition of this new awareness of the significance of walking for much daily activity, models of future trip generation and modal split have been developed with the individual as the 'unit' for analysis, in order to take account of these variations. The primary objective has become the safe, efficient and convenient movement of people rather than of traffic. Nevertheless, the significance of the land use pattern for accessibility, particularly on foot, and for the linkages between facilities is not always realised—in spite of the phrase 'land use' in the generic title of these studies. Moreover, the potential of walking for reducing motorised traffic and as a competing mode in modelling future transport systems, does not get fully developed.

As a consequence, there is no knowledge of how the allocation of priority to walking would meet the objective of 'providing for the safe, efficient and convenient movement of people' nor to what extent such priority would 'interfere' with the safe, efficient and convenient movement of people travelling by motorised means.

The principal means for evaluating the alternative options proposed in transport plans is cost-benefit analysis, the principal features of which, on the benefit side, are the savings in vehicle running costs, motorised travel time and road accidents. To date, no attempt has been made to integrate walking fully into this analysis by looking at the effects of various transport policy options and traffic management measures on walking and on people's capacity to meet their travel needs economically on foot. Neither has there been examination of the potentially *beneficial* effects of walking, which are not shared by motor travel, and which could be included in cost-benefit analysis—energy savings (including the effects of the reduction in oil imports on the balance of payments), health benefits (attributable to the preventive medical aspects of regular walking), improved environmental quality (the reduction in vehicular noise and pollution), and so on.

Indeed, the most recent comprehensive attempt to treat with this subject[15]

---

[14]Perhaps the best example of these Mark II LUTs is Wytconsult, *West Yorkshire Transportation Studies—Final Report,* Vols 1-4, (1977).

[15]A. Lassière, *The Environmental Evaluation of Transport Plans,* Department of the Environment, (1976).

has been limited to recommending the quantification of traffic impact on pedestrians—danger, exposure to unpleasant conditions and delay in crossing roads—in particular locations rather than in a strategic context.[16]

Transport Research

Official attitudes to a subject affecting the public in their day-to-day lives can also be examined through the medium of research. Studies conducted or sponsored by government bodies or agencies reflect the view prevailing at the time regarding the significance, appropriateness and worthiness of the subject for the limited expertise and funds available in a particular field. The principal source of technical and scientific fact for use in formulating and implementing government policy on transport is the Department of Transport's own research wing—the Transport and Road Research Laboratory (TRRL).[17] Most of its completed studies are reported in its Laboratory Report (LR) and Supplementary Report (SR) series. A review of the research in which it has been engaged over the last decade suggests that the earlier strong orientation towards road transport research—road construction, traffic problems, public transport and road safety (including the exposure of pedestrians to accident risk)—has been somewhat modified. In recent years, changes have been made in the structure of the Laboratory through the creation of the Access and Mobility Division within the Transport Operations Department; as its title suggests, this Division is concerned with all transport modes, including walking.

However, there has not been a commensurate change in its professional staff—the forte of its scientists has been predominantly in the field of sophisticated technology. Planning and associated disciplines are strongly under-represented. A count of research studies over the last few years suggests that scant attention has been given to pedestrians other than a large programme related to their safety. The current Annual Report (for 1977) describes more than 100 studies of which only one is concerned specifically with pedestrians; this is focussed on their behaviour at road crossings in order to establish acceptable time delays for them. Moreover, a closer look at past studies which have been concerned with the convenience of pedestrian travel reveals, with one or two notable exceptions, a somewhat reduced significance with respect to its being viewed as research *for* such travel. A study of pedestrian (and cycle) journeys was undertaken to establish the potential patronage for new forms of public transport; another one was concerned with pedestrian interference with traffic flow, whilst a third after acknowledging the need for a new approach to transport policy to take account of 'walk access', nevertheless discussed the problem of encouraging people to walk from bus stops close to town centres rather than from adjacent car parks. The current Annual Report describes a study of old age pensioners' travel without

---

[16]As far as the authors know, no assessment has been made of the likely costs and benefits of a wide range of inconveniences in encouraging people to transfer from walking to travel by bus or car.

[17]Before 1973 its simpler title of *Road Research Laboratory* reflected the type of research carried on within it.

mentioning that over half the recorded journeys in the survey were made on foot.

Further expression of this lacuna with regard to walking can be seen in the forecasts of future traffic levels upon which much of transport policy has been based. It might be salutary for these forecasts to incorporate estimates of future levels of pedestrian travel, particularly if the levels were disaggregated according to different social groups in the population. Indeed, there are grounds for believing that the accuracy of such forecasts would be considerably higher than those made regarding motor traffic over the last fifteen years. The lacuna is reflected too in the composition of the TRRL's Advisory Committee on Transport none of whose 14 members has any special interest in pedestrians or pedestrian travel. It is also reflected in the Department of Transport's Library Bulletin the contents of which have no section for walking or pedestrian movement. Analysis of the articles, books, conference proceedings and so on, listed in it reveals again that where walking is reported it is principally in the context of the safety aspects and the planning of precincts and only very rarely also in the context of modal split—though pedestrians do have the distinction of being classified as 'road users'.

Research studies in universities and institutes concerned with transport reflect the principal concerns of these same bodies in their capacity as sponsors of research—there is a disproportionate investment in research on motorised travel. Walking is a subject area for studies of pedestrian safety—exposure risk, accident and traffic conflicts—and necessary though this is, it does not cover all the requirements of pedestrians. In the last two years a study of pedestrian habits has been commissioned of the Office of Population Censuses and Surveys. It aims to establish the risks that pedestrians take so as to aid the safety campaign; the study's potential use in planning for pedestrian travel is limited.

It seems somewhat bizarre that where studies are focussed on pedestrian movement *per se*, they are often in the context of relatively extreme situations of pedestrian traffic jams on pavements or of determining appropriate dimensions for footways or underpasses. Such studies are generally explored on a scientific rather than a social scientific plane. Studies concerned with pedestrian convenience and environment are few and far between, though there are notable exceptions.[18] Indeed, one has to look abroad to read of studies concerned with tolerable distances that people are prepared to walk in different circumstances, or with the influence of weather or of environmental quality.

Public Attitudes

One factor that could account for this state of affairs is that no political party has considered the subject worthy of incorporation into its manifesto—as

---

[18]See John Elkington, Roger McGlynn and John Roberts, *The Pedestrian: Planning and Research,* Transport and Environment Studies, 1976, for a review; and the works of P. B. Goodwin while at the Traffic Studies Group, University College, London, and the Department of Planning and Transportation, Greater London Council.

is the case, for instance, with regard to the maintenance of an effective public transport system. Indeed, the only organisation campaigning on behalf of pedestrians is the Pedestrians Association for Road Safety but its membership is relatively small and its objectives have been, as its name since its foundation in 1929 indicates, primarily concerned with road safety rather than with all aspects of public policy affecting pedestrians.[19]

In recent years other organisations such as Friends of the Earth, Transport 2000, Age Concern and the London Amenity and Transport Association have chosen to voice their concern about such matters as the deterioration in the conditions in which people get around on foot and the erosion of opportunities for people to meet their daily travel needs in this way. The Royal Society for the Prevention of Accidents, of course continues its programme of seeking to encourage the adoption of measures aimed at reducing all types of accident, including those in which pedestrians are involved.

Nevertheless it is sobering to consider that the loss of life and limb among pedestrians each year—over 20,000 are killed or seriously injured—may be occurring partly because policy makers are not sufficiently informed of the relative risks of using different travel methods and of the already proven ways of reducing road accidents, (for instance, by the introduction and enforcement of lower speed limits), to enable them to promote more corrective life-saving measures, and partly because such solutions have not been seen to be politically worthy of adoption. One reason for this could be a presumption that the 'public' does not lightly acquiesce to intrusion on its freedom. It may also be that, for whatever reason, politicians are not sufficiently pressured by public opinion. Indeed, the fact that the separate statement on proposed legislation to improve road safety, which was promised in the 1977 White Paper on Transport Policy, has not materialised seems to reflect a surprising inertia given the urgency with which legislation is introduced to prevent loss of life in other areas of the economy.

Regrettably, people are killed and injured on the roads in a fairly random, geographical pattern so that the impact is diffused. Moreover, the very fact that accidents occur so frequently seems to dull instinctive responses of sympathy, and demands for ameliorisation of the situation then become more apathetic. Additionally, the media often see their function more to capture the public imagination than to inform it. As a consequence, front page headlines and photographs are used to dramatise the horrific loss of life in an air or train crash (both of which occur extremely infrequently but with relatively large numbers of people involved), but only a few column inches are devoted to each *year's* toll of death on the roads. The statistics are then presented with a degree of cold bloodedness more appropriate to statistics on annual rainfall.

The reaction of the operators of the country's transport system mirrors the response of the media. A public inquiry is immediately instituted to establish causation in the case of an air or train crash followed by the publication of the

---

[19]Nevertheless, it has recently decided to extend its sphere of activity overtly to embrace the wider aspects of policy on pedestrian travel, and in recognition of this, to limit its name to *The Pedestrians Association*.

findings, whilst a road crash is dealt with through a local police investigation, and a coroner's inquest records a verdict. On the other hand, the preparedness of government to take strong action in the interests of personal safety is reflected in the financial support given to British Rail a large part of which, it could be argued, is effectively used to maintain its enviable record on the safety of train travel.

It may be concluded from this review of the consideration given to walking that, as a means of travel, it has received scant or superficial attention in legislation, policy and research, particularly at the level of strategic thinking and policy development. The safety aspects of travel on foot, however, have justifiably received much attention and have been the subject of a considerable amount of public concern, though the approach and focus can sometimes be questioned insofar as these reflect attitudes towards the relative convenience of walking and motor travel as well as their safety. Three questions stem from this: the first is just how significant is walking as a method of travel; secondly, whose interests are not being sufficiently represented; and thirdly, do the answers to these two questions suggest the need for change in current policy and practice?

II The Pattern and Safety of Walking

It has been seen that walking has been conventionally viewed as a means of travel of little relevance to the transport planner. It has been primarily in the situations of potential conflict of pedestrians crossing roads planned for mechanical transport that attention has been paid to the character of journeys made on foot in order to ensure both the maximum safety of pedestrians and the minimum delay to traffic. Some explanation for this predilection for only one facet of pedestrian travel has been due no doubt to a lack of knowledge of the characteristics of walking. Recently, however, there have been indications of its recognition as an element of transport.[1] But just how significant is it within the spectrum of total personal travel?

The Extent of Walking

In fact, as Table II.I shows, there is an impressive array of activity undertaken on foot—about one journey per person each day and over one in three of all the journeys that people make on average.[2] This is only a slightly lower proportion than that for car travel, and far higher than for all other methods of travel, including public transport. Indeed, it amounts to over 48 million journeys being made on foot each day in Britain.

The total extent of walking also includes, of course, the beginning and end stages of journeys defined as being by car or public transport. If all journeys are disaggregated into their separate stages then the significance of walking is increased to a 49 per cent share, compared with 35 per cent for the car and only 12 per cent for public transport.

As discussed in the previous chapter, the significance of walking is, however, diminished in the three volumes of the National Travel Survey (NTS) analysis so far published by the Department of Transport, for the record in these volumes excludes journeys which were made on foot if they were less

---

[1] For instance the 1977 White Paper on *Transport Policy* stated in para. 35 that 'For the future, therefore we should aim to decrease our absolute dependence on transport . . . and to plan more consciously for those who walk as well as those who use mechanised transport'.

[2] As noted in the introduction, respondents were asked not to record journeys of less than 50 yards, a distance which could cover a small but not insignificant proportion of visits to shops, public houses, neighbours and so on.

Table II.1 Modal split on all journeys

	Walk	Car	Bus/ train	Cycle	Other	N/a*	All journeys†
			Per cent				
All journeys	35.2	39.5	11.3	3.2	1.2	9.6	100
Trip rate:			*Number*				
Journeys per day per person‡	0.90	1.01	0.29	0.08	0.03	0.24	2.56

    * See Appendix A, para. 7.
    † Total number of journeys — 71,474.
    ‡ Number of people included (aged 3 years and over) — 27,906.

than one mile long. Table II.2 shows that this misleadingly deflates the proportion of walk journeys by a factor of 3 and thereby inflates that of all other travel methods. Indeed, this distorting procedure results in the exclusion of 25 per cent of all personal travel. It is made all the more illogical because journeys under one mile by other methods are included.

Table II.2 Comparison of modal split excluding and including walk journeys of under one mile

	Walk	Car	Bus/ train	Other	N/a	All journeys
			Per cent			
Modal split **excluding** walks of less than 1 mile	12.4	59.9	19.6	6.1	2.0	100
Modal split **including** walks of less than 1 mile	35.2	39.5	11.3	4.4	9.6	100

A further effect of this exclusion is that a not insignificant proportion of people are wrongly deemed as having made no journeys at all during the week of the survey. The published 1972/73 findings report that 11 per cent of respondents made no journeys, a proportion which rises to 14 per cent for people under 16 years and to a staggering 33 per cent for women over 65 years—a finding which, it it were true, would indicate a disturbing level of isolation among this relatively vulnerable population group. Likewise, many other people are deemed to have made only one or two journeys a week, whereas in reality they might have been no less active, albeit locally and on foot, than their car 'dependent' neighbours travelling both locally and further afield, on four wheels. The result of this is the production of a totally false picture of relative activity levels among the population at large.

Distance

The reason for the extent of this distortion is that almost three-quarters of walk journeys are less than one mile long. (The great majority of the remainder are one to two miles in length.) Journeys under one mile by all travel methods account for about one-third of *all* journeys, (considerably more than the one in five journeys in the one to two-mile band) and almost 90 per cent of them are made on foot. No other distance band covers as much travel, as Table II.3 indicates. Thus journeys for distances of two miles or more by *all* travel methods are in the minority though, as will be seen later, they are of much more consequence when measured against total mileage travelled.

Table II.3   Travel method and distance, in miles

	Walk:			Car:		Bus/		
Less than 1 mile	1 mile but less than 2 miles	2 or more miles	Less than 2 miles	2 or more miles	train †	Other †	N/a* †
Per cent						*Per cent*		
All journeys								
25	8	2	10	30	11	4	10

† All distances
* See Appendix A, para. 7.

A finer breakdown of walk journeys reveals that 40 per cent are less than half a mile long.[3] These represent one in six of all journeys—more than equivalent in number to all public transport journeys, of any distance. Indeed, over 20 per cent of walk journeys are less than a quarter of a mile long—a distance band that may appear to encompass too few journeys to be of much importance until it is realised that these short walk journeys are equivalent to ten times the number of rail journeys over all distances.

The average length of journeys is useful in indicating the wide variation in the typical 'catchment of opportunity' available by the different travel methods. Thus the average (mean) length of walk journeys of about four-fifths of a mile can encompass an area of 2.4 square miles—the size of a small town—whereas the average car journey of nine miles is ten times longer but provides potential access over an area one hundred times greater—240 square miles. Estimates of total mileage travelled in the NTS lack precision as distance is recorded in broad bands, especially for longer journeys. However, if the mid-point of each band is taken as the average, then it can be calculated that the daily distance travelled totals almost 370,000 miles, that is 13 miles per

---

[3] It should be recalled that the 1975/76 NTS excluded walk journeys of under 50 yards—probably two or three per cent of all walk journeys.

person. Over 20,000 of these miles are on foot; this represents about 6 per cent of all miles travelled, though accounting for 35 per cent of all journeys.[4]

Travel Time

Although journeys on foot are much shorter in distance than those by other travel methods, there is less variation among methods in terms of travel time because of the much slower speed of walking; Table II.4 shows this. The figures suggest perhaps that people are somewhat less inclined to spend time on a walk journey compared with a motorised one, in all likelihood because of the physical effort involved, and because an extra few minutes walked makes little difference to the range of opportunities reached, unlike an extra few minutes travelling in a car. In fact, the average (mean) time spent on a walking journey is about 18 minutes and on a motorised journey about 24 minutes.

Table II.4   Travel time on walk and non-walk journeys

Travel time	Per cent of walk journeys in each time band	Per cent of journeys by other methods in each time band	Walk journeys as per cent of all journeys in each time band
Less than 15 minutes	53	37	45
15—29 minutes	33	34	36
30—44 minutes	10	16	28
45—59 minutes	2	5	17
60 minutes or more	2	8	12
All times	100	100	37

In common with calculations of mileage travelled in the NTS, calculations of time spent travelling are subject to some inaccuracy as time intervals of fifteen minutes are employed—and the first of these encompasses half of all walk journeys. If the mid-point of each interval is taken as the average, however, an approximation of total time travelling can be calculated, showing that people travel for about one hour daily of which one quarter is spent walking.

Journey Purpose

Particular types of journey are very much associated with walking. Figure 2.1 shows that, of essential journeys, a high proportion of those to and from shops and school are made on foot but the proportions for travel to, from or in the course of work are low; of optional journeys, those for informal recreation have the highest proportion made on foot—that is about two thirds. However, in view of the fact that some journeys are made more frequently than others, it can be seen that shopping on foot accounts for nearly one-tenth

---

[4]Car journeys account for 74 per cent of miles travelled and 45 per cent of journeys; public transport journeys account for about 17 per cent of miles travelled and 15 per cent of journeys.

of all personal travel—a figure that, in terms of journey purpose combined with travel method is exceeded only (and only just) by car travel to and from work. Because of the high frequency of work journeys, walking to work is significant in the context of all personal travel, even if not in the sole context of travel to work.

Figure 2.1 Journeys on foot as proportion of all journeys, by purpose

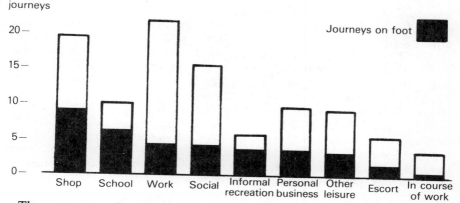

The average number of journeys per person per day can be calculated for all respondents in respect of shopping, social and leisure journeys, but for work and school journeys it is more appropriate to calculate the rate only for the employed and school children respectively. Table II.5 shows these rates together with the average rates for journeys made on foot.

Table II.5 Number of journeys on foot and by all methods, by journey purpose

Journey purpose*	Journeys per person per day:	
	Walk	All methods
Education	0.76	1.28
Work	0.24	1.24
Shopping	0.23	0.49
Social visits	0.10	0.39
Recreation†	0.10	0.18
Personal business	0.09	0.24
Escorting	0.04	0.14
Eat/drink	0.03	0.08
Entertainment	0.03	0.09
Sport	0.01	0.06

* Sample sizes: Education, n = 5,509 children, aged 5-15 years
   Work, n = 12,510 employed adults
   Other journey purposes, n = 27,906 respondents
† Includes holidays

23

The distorting effect of excluding walk journeys of under one mile, as in the published tables of the NTS, is clearly greater for those journey purposes for which walking represents the more frequent travel method. For instance, it results in only half the school journeys and only two-thirds of the shopping journeys being recorded. The effect of this, in turn, can be that changes in the pattern of these journeys are not as conspicuous as, say, changes in journey patterns which are motor-orientated.

Variation by Time of Day, Week and Year

The extent to which people walk on their day-to-day travel varies at different times of the day, week and year. The influence of these temporal changes is more easily gauged on optional journeys. There is a small increase in the rate and length of walk journeys at the weekend and when there is more time available, and in the months from June to August when the longer hours of daylight, the warmer temperatures and the drier weather are likely to encourage activity outside the home. On the other hand, there is a fairly marked increase both in the proportion and number of walk journeys on weekdays compared with the weekend and this increase also occurs at specific times of the day. From 9 am to 12 am, and from about 3 pm to 5 pm when most school and shopping journeys are made, nearly half of all journeys are made on foot, whereas in the evening the proportion drops to well under one third. In both instances, these differences are largely accounted for by the lesser availability of cars during working hours to the majority of people (even in car owning households) and by the more local character of much activity at these times—and, of course, by the earlier bedtimes of some of those more dependent on walking.

Comparison of 1972/73 and 1975/76

Overall, the number of journeys per person recorded on the final day of the survey was 11 per cent less in 1975/76 than in 1972/73 : 2.56 compared with 2.87. The decline between the two surveys can be explained partly by the higher numbers of rural and elderly respondents in the later survey, but this accounts for only part of the decline, as further analysis shows a reduction in *all* types of area and all age groups. The recorded decline was proportionately twice as high for walking as for all travel methods, as Table II.6 shows.

Table II.6   Walking in relation to all travel, 1972/73 and 1975/76

| | Number of journeys per person per day: | | Journeys |
	Walk	All methods	on foot
			Per cent
1972/73	1.15	2.87	40
1975/76	0.90	2.56	35
Per cent change	− 22	− 11	

The change in modal split is difficult to measure because in the later survey, travel method was not recorded for ten per cent of journeys made on the final day (in the earlier survey it was one per cent). However, as far as can be seen from examination of the other characteristics of these journeys, it is reasonable to assume that they were in fact motorised, and more likely to be made by car than by public transport, probably in the ratio of 6:4. This assumption means that the number of journeys per person by car increased by about ten per cent, but by public transport it decreased by the same amount.[5] The use of bicycles also increased slightly. Any transfer of walk journeys would therefore seem to be to car travel (and to a much less degree, to cycling) rather than to public transport.

Journeys recorded in 1975/76 were longer in distance and time than those recorded in 1972/73, and this is true for walking and for all methods of travel combined—though in both surveys over 30 per cent of all journeys were under one mile, and of these, well over four in five were made on foot. The change in walking was complex, with decreases in both the shortest and longest journeys and increases—relatively and absolutely—in the medium distance walks of between one and two miles. Table II.7 shows this.

Table II.7   Distance walked—comparison between 1972/73 and 1975/76

	Journeys on foot		Journeys per person per day (all travel methods)	
	1972/73	1975/76	1972/73	1975/76
	Per cent		*Number*	
Less than ¼ mile	28	22	0.32	0.20
¼ mile but less than ½ mile	23	21	0.27	0.19
½ mile but less than 1 mile	27	29	0.31	0.26
1 mile but less than 2 miles	14	23	0.16	0.21
2 miles or more	8	5	0.09	0.05

It is possible that the change shown in the table reflects a two-fold process, one part being a lengthening of some originally short walk journeys, the other being a transfer of walk journeys. In particular the longer walk journeys may have been transferred to car travel—the car journey then being made to the same *or* to a more distant destination. The table indicates that the observed decline in walking does not stem from the change in survey methodology between the two surveys which led to the exclusion of all walks of less than 50 yards in 1975/76. No doubt this accounted for some of the decline in the very short journeys of under a quarter of a mile, but it is unlikely to account for all of this and cannot, of course, account for any of the decline in journeys of other lengths.

---

[5] The number of journeys per person per day by car was recorded in the National Travel Survey of 1972/73 and 1975/76 as 1.15 and 1.26 respectively; the number of journeys by public transport in those years was 0.42 and 0.39 respectively.

Though both long and short journeys decreased, the long ones were few in number and so the overall balance was a lengthening of walk journey and an increase in travel time. The median walk time rose by 2 minutes per journey, from about 12 to about 14 minutes, with the proportion of walk journeys lasting at least 15 minutes rising from 39 per cent to 47 per cent. The average (mean) time rose from 16 to 18 minutes; this increase may appear small in terms of its absolute time value, but it should be recalled that it represents a *daily* increase *per person* and so, if it were to be costed as in traditional transport planning exercises, it would represent a substantial figure equivalent to the cost of nearly two million hours a day, nationally.

The distribution of journey purposes shows relatively little change between the two surveys, though the pattern of journeys changed for each purpose, as Table II.8 shows. The number and proportion of walk journeys per person fell for each purpose, except for journeys made while escorting someone else—taking a child to school or an elderly person on a hospital visit and so on. These changes are discussed in more detail in later sections.

Table II.8   Significance of walking for each journey purpose, 1972/73 and 1975/76

Journey purpose	Per cent of journeys made on foot	
	1972/73 NTS	1975/76 NTS
Education	67	60
Recreation	61	57
Shopping	56	46
Eat/drink	50	42
Personal business	41	38
Escorting	29	29
Entertainment	34	29
Social visits	32	27
Sport	30	23
Work	22	19

The Safety of Pedestrians

The wealth of statistics on road accidents is a reflection of the influence of organisations associated with the interests of pedestrians, of the involvement of the police in so many criminal proceedings relating to road accidents, and of public concern generally. The scale and scope of research at the Transport and Road Research Laboratory, with its commendable focus on children's safety, is also indicative of a strong desire to prevent these accidents occurring in such large numbers. In recent years over 2,000 people have been killed annually when walking on the public highway, and over 18,000 seriously injured. These pedestrian casualties account for one in three of all deaths in road accidents and about one in four of all serious injuries;[6] most result from pedestrians being knocked down by a motor vehicle when crossing the road. In addition a further 50,000 pedestrians are recorded as being slightly injured to the extent that they require hospital treatment.

But even with this figure there are a number of reasons why the total of pedestrian casualties may not be accurately represented. For instance, an accident involving the driver of a motor vehicle and a pedestrian is less likely to be reported to the police if the pedestrian feels, or is encouraged to feel, at fault, and also if the vehicle is not damaged and the driver does not, therefore, have to make a claim on his insurance policy. In addition, published statistics do not include those injured if it is the result of a fall on the pavement due, for instance, to icy conditions, or to tripping on the kerb or on a badly maintained flagstone.[7] It could be noted here that in a study of personal mobility of housewives and pensioners, pavements of inadequate width or poor condition were cited most frequently to account for the difficulties of getting around on foot rather than the difficulty of crossing roads.[8]

However, there has been a progressive reduction in pedestrian casualties so that now it is three-quarters of the annual total of ten years ago. Clearly one of the more compelling issues facing transport planners to-day is to continue with the promotion of accident-saving measures which have contributed to this reduction. To do so, and to do it with a degree of priority compatible with the number of casualties, requires appreciation of when and how and where the accidents occur. Moreover, it is desirable to relate them to the pattern of pedestrian activity.

It is only fairly recently that analysis of this kind has been possible because, as has been seen, national data on walking journeys has only been available since 1974.[9] Figure 2.2 shows that recorded pedestrian casualties rise and fall more in consonance with the rise and fall of motorised journeys than of journeys on foot, the incidence of accidents reflecting the incidence of situations of conflict between pedestrians and drivers. For instance, during the morning and evening rush hours the likelihood of a pedestrian accident occurring is higher than at other times of the day.

Another significant feature is the marked increase in pedestrian casualties, in spite of the decline in the number of journeys on foot, in the late evening and on Fridays, and on Saturdays compared with Sundays. Statistics by hour of day and day of week on the proportion of drivers involved in accidents who had positive breath tests would appear to confirm that this is partly due to the effect of drinking on drivers,[10] though no doubt drunken pedestrians are also

---

[6] Department of Transport, *Road Accidents, Great Britain,* op. cit. Table 4.

[7] The equivalent omission for mechanised travellers would be to exclude those road casualties where only one vehicle was involved.

[8] Hillman et al. *Transport Realities and Planning Policy,* op. cit.

[9] The first year when 1972/73 National Travel Survey data could be examined.

[10] Department of Transport, *Road Accidents, 1977,* HMSO, (1978), Table 40.

Figure 2.2 Daily journey rates and fatal and serious pedestrian casualties according to day of week, time of day and month

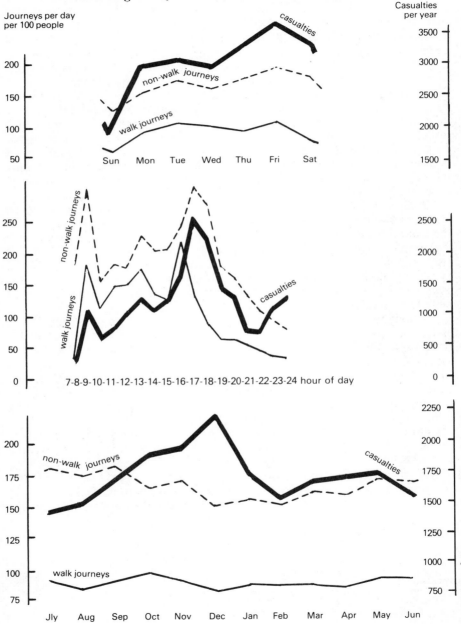

to blame.[11] The impairment of a person's judgement after drinking too may explain why pedestrian deaths and serious injuries in December are higher than those in adjacent months, and why the injuries are more often fatal. The data suggest also that in many instances a factor contributing to the increase in accidents later in the day and in the week may be explained by a greater proneness to carelessness at these times when both drivers and pedestrians are more likely to be tired.

A further explanation for the rise in pedestrian casualties in the winter and late evenings is the poorer visibility owing to darkness, fog and the lower light intensity generally at these times. In addition, there is the greater likelihood of ice on the roads and of skidding in the winter. In fact, the incidence of road accidents in which a vehicle skids is about three times higher in the months of October to March as from April to September.[12]

In contrast to statistics published on casualty rates for mechanised travel, which are calculated from traffic surveys and related to miles travelled, there are no equivalent statistics on the casualty rates for pedestrians related to the distance they walk or the time they spend walking, both of which could be considered as better measures of exposure risk. However, a fairly close estimate of these rates can be obtained by using NTS data on the frequency, time and length of journeys made by each travel method, grossing these up for

Table II.9   Road accident rates, 1976, according to different methods of personal travel*

Method of travel	per 100,000 journeys	Accident rate: per 100,000 hours	per 100,000 vehicle kilometres	Fatal/serious accidents	
				Number	*Per cent*
Bus	2.4	4.6	2.9	1,240	2
Walk†	11.5	40.2	82.6	20,630	25
Car	17.3	42.3	12.3	34,879	43
Cycle	30.1	111.8	104.2	4,931	6
2-wheel motor	405.1	568.8	442.1	19,851	24
All methods	17.9	48.3	22.5	81,531	100

* Calculated from annual rates in Department of Transport, *Road Accidents Great Britain 1976*, HMSO (1977), Table 47

† Calculated by relating the rate per person to the frequency with which the NTS shows journeys made on foot.

[11] Analysis of the pattern of drinking offences shows that there were twice as many proceedings against pedestrians charged with drunkenness as against motorists. Twenty Fifth Annual Report of the Christian Economic and Social Research Foundation on the Chief Constables' Reports, England and Wales and Scotland for 1977. Part One, Drink Offences, (1978) page 4.

[12] Department of Transport, *Road Accidents Great Britain 1976*, HMSO (1977), Table 42.

the whole population, and then relating them to the pattern of road accidents in the year of the survey. It can be seen in Table II.9 that the accident rate per journey and per hour spent travelling is somewhat lower for car travellers than for pedestrians, but that in mileage terms, walking is much more hazardous. Perhaps not surprisingly in view of pedestrians' vulnerability, both their fatality and injury rates per kilometre are far higher than those for the drivers of cars or goods vehicles—the principal road users involved when pedestrians are injured.[13] Whilst at first sight it may appear that the rates for people travelling on two-wheeled vehicles are higher still, it should perhaps be borne in mind that, were the calculation more appropriately related solely to the miles travelled by pedestrians when they are most at risk, that is almost exclusively when crossing roads, it could confidently be predicted that pedestrian rates would well exceed even these. Not only is the accident rate per kilometre far higher for pedestrians than for people travelling by car or bus, but the pedestrian is also twice as likely to be killed.[14]

It would appear that the severity, if not the number of pedestrian casualties is markedly reduced when lower speed limits are adopted. Analysis of the effects on road accidents of the temporary lowering of the speed limit in 1974 as part of the Government's energy saving campaign showed this to result in fewer accidents.[15] Another source also provides some indication of the effect of reducing traffic speed: on roads in London with 70 mph, 50 mph, 40 mph and 30 mph speed limits respectively, the proportions of pedestrian casualties which are fatal or serious are 46 per cent, 33 per cent, 35 per cent and 21 per cent.[16] At lower speed limits, this progression would presumably continue.

Thus walking is a considerable component of daily travel, similar, in fact, to the car in terms of frequency of 'use'. Indeed, it predominates in numbers over all other travel methods combined for all journeys up to five miles long, and is particularly significant for travel to school, shops and for informal recreation. Comparison of data from the two National Travel Surveys has shown that fewer journeys were made on foot in the later survey, though the time taken and the distance walked is longer. It has been seen, too, that walking is significant in another respect, for when calculated in terms of hours of exposure to traffic, it is as hazardous as car travel, and in terms of distance travelled, it is far more hazardous than car or public transport travel.

---

[13] Cars are involved in three quarters of all accidents in which there is a pedestrian casualty (Metropolitan Police, private communication with the authors).

[14] Of pedestrian casualties, 3.4 per cent are fatal in contrast to 1.7 per cent of casualties of people travelling by car and 0.5 per cent of those travelling by bus. (Department of Transport, op. cit., Table 4).

[15] Nevertheless, as a result of the representations made by the motor and freight industries the limit was returned to its original level in 1977.

[16] Metropolitan Police, *Personal Injury Road Accidents: a statistical analysis for 1977*, New Scotland Yard, Table 42.

III Patterns of Walking in The Population

The previous chapter has shown the pattern of walking within the overall spectrum of personal travel. Clearly part of the variation in the extent of walking compared with other travel is attributable to the locations of the people and places that are visited. Some of them entail only short journeys that can easily be made on foot — children to primary school and playground, housewives to local shops, or pensioners to the post-office; others necessitate resort to the car, bus or train to get to the town centre, the countryside and so on. This variation in walking by type of journey is examined in some detail in later chapters; this chapter focuses on the variation by type of person. It looks at all journeys together, only occasionally distinguishing between essential and optional journeys[1], and asks the basic questions of who walks, how much, and how far.

At the risk of presenting what might seem sometimes rather obvious findings, the chapter quantifies the answers in some detail, firstly in order to show whose interests are being glossed over in the sophisticated world of transport planning, traffic management and strategic land use planning exercises. Secondly, the analysis is necessary so that evaluation of this neglect can take account of how important those interests are to the travelling lives of the people concerned and, indeed, of how important they are to their lives in general, bearing in mind that the travel itself is on the whole a means of attaining some necessary or preferred activity. And thirdly, if these interests are to feature in planning more strongly in the future, then this basic analysis is clearly needed to help identify priorities and assess the likely effects of plans and policies. After examining the profile of pedestrians and showing how walking features in their day-to-day travel, the chapter looks briefly at the sombre side of their preference for or reliance on walking by showing to what extent different types of pedestrians are involved in road accidents.

A person's propensity to walk is associated directly or indirectly with a variety of personal and social characteristics, such as age, sex, income, social class, the availability of other travel methods and the opportunity and

---

[1]In this study, work, school, shopping and personal business journeys have been classified as essential and the rest as optional — that is predominantly for leisure purposes.

convenience of using them. The NTS allows examination of a number of these variables and some of the effects of their interaction on travel.

Car Ownership and Licence Holding

Two thirds of the NTS respondents lived in car owning households, including one in six in households with two or more cars, and just over one third held a driving licence; thus, one third were without a car or licence and a further third, not being able to drive, could not individually use their household's car. Car ownership, naturally, affects people's travel patterns — not only in relation to transfers between public transport and the car, but also in relation to the amount of walking they do and their reliance on pedestrian access. Table III.1 shows the extent of this influence: the proportion of journeys made on foot is twice as high among people in households without a car compared with those in car owning households. In numerical terms, they make about three journeys on foot to every two reported by those with a household car. This situation is, however, reversed when journeys by all methods are assessed; those with a household car make more journeys altogether than do people without one. A similar pattern exisits between people with and without a driving licence — people with no driving licence walk more than those with one but have a lower level of activity overall.[2]

Table III.1   Daily journey rates and modal split, by household car ownership and personal licence holding

	Journeys per person per day:			Journeys on foot
	on foot	motorised †	all methods	
	Number			*Per cent*
Cars in household:*				
Two or more	0.60	2.45	3.05	20
One	0.88	1.45	2.83	31
None	1.07	0.91	2.01	53
All households	0.91	1.67	2.58	35
Licence holder	0.60	2.65	3.25	18
Non-licence holder	1.07	1.16	2.23	48

* Includes light vans and three-wheeled vehicles.
† Includes cycling.

Thus, walking features strongly in the lives of people without full access to a car[3]. Children and pensioners[4] make about half their journeys on foot, that is almost double the proportion made by adults of working age, and consequently their share of all walk journeys is over two fifths of the total,

---

[2]Eighty one per cent of the adult respondents in households with two or more cars were licence holders compared with 63 per cent of those with one car and 12 per cent of those in households without a car.
[3]Appendix C shows the variation in car ownership and licence-holding according to age and sex.
[4]Children aged 3—15; men pensioners 65 years and over; women pensioners 60 years and over.

whereas their share of the population is less than one third. There is also a marked difference by sex, particularly among people of working age, with women walking far more than men.

Age and Sex

Table III.2 shows the variation in the extent of walking according to age and sex in more detail, indicating how a focus on motorised travel is tantamount to giving very uneven attention to the travel of different groups. The group making most journeys, but the lowest proportion of them on foot — that is only one in five — are men between the ages of 21 and 60; women in the same age group make almost double that proportion. The marked similarity in the high proportion of journeys on foot of men and women pensioners reflects their more common level of access to a car and also the more common geographical base in which they circulate; few men pensioners have a journey to work, which for younger men generally entails motorised travel.

Table III.2 Daily journey rates and modal split, by age group and sex

| | Journeys per person per day: | | | Journeys |
	on foot	motorised *	all methods	on foot
		Number		*Per cent*
Men:				
aged 16—20 years	0.87	2.17	3.04	29
aged 21—29 years	0.67	2.59	3.26	21
aged 30—59 years	0.61	2.58	3.19	19
aged 60—64 years	0.80	1.90	2.70	30
All men aged 16—64 years	0.67	2.47	3.14	21
Women:				
aged 16—20 years	0.96	1.91	2.87	34
aged 21—29 years	1.12	1.75	2.81	40
aged 30—59 years	0.95	1.70	2.65	36
All women aged 16—59 years	0.99	1.71	2.70	37
Pensioners:				
men aged 65 +	0.84	1.06	1.90	44
women aged 60 +	0.72	0.79	1.51	48
All pensioners	0.76	0.88	1.64	46
Children and young teenagers:				
aged 3—4 years	0.94	1.06	2.00	47
aged 5—10 years	1.23	0.99	2.22	55
aged 11—15 years	1.28	1.40	2.68	48
All children aged 3—15 years	1.21	1.16	2.37	51

* Includes cycling.

It can be seen too that children not only make most of their journeys on foot but also make a significantly higher number of journeys on foot than older people. The variation that occurs with each additional year of childhood and adolescence is particularly interesting: as Figure 3.1 shows, there is a decline in

Figure 3.1   Modal split according to age*, 1972/73

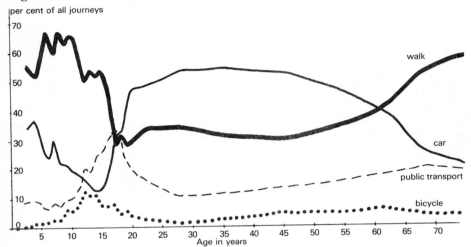

*The 1972/73 NTS has been used for this figure as it is only in this survey that respondents gave their precise age up to 20 years old.

the proportion of journeys on foot around the age of 11 coinciding with the time when children begin to travel a greater distance to secondary school, a journey more likely to require the use of public transport. The further lurch downwards in the amount of walking in the teenage years from the age of 15 coincides with increased motorised travel, to work and leisure, presumably sometimes as passengers in the cars of somewhat older friends. It can be seen that, from the age of 17 to 18, when teenagers can begin to exercise choice in their use of travel modes, the pattern of walking stabilises whilst car travel is increasingly substituted for public transport travel. As the levels of household car ownership throughout childhood and adolescence are fairly constant, the sharp changes in the modal split over a relatively short number of years also confirm that access to the so-called 'household car' varies considerably with age. It also varies by sex — women being more dependent than their husbands on walking. In later years, walking regains the upper hand for both men and women while car and public transport use coverge again. This results from the financial constraints of retirement, the high proportion of women pensioners and also the fact that today's pensioners have not lived through a period in their lives when being able to drive was as commonplace as it is today.

Variations in walking within age and sex group also reflect motorised mobility and compound the simpler variation which is evident in analysis by either car ownership or age and sex. For each age and sex group there is an

34

increase in the extent of walking with a decrease in access to a car, especially as regards essential journeys to work, school, shops, clinics, post offices, and so on. Overall activity rates also vary; the extent of travel by all methods falls as the extent of walking rises. Hence, a heavy reliance on walking is reflected in fewer journeys being made. This means that the proportion of journeys made on foot, indicating the significance of pedestrian access to the travel of each group, varies substantially within groups of people at the same stage in life, as well as between groups at different stages. These variations are shown in Table III.3 and Figure 3.2.

Figure 3.2   Proportion of journeys on foot according to age group, sex, and household car ownership, 1975/76

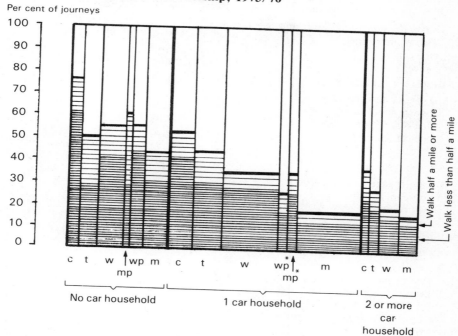

Note: width of column relates to proportion of the total journeys made by the population within each category.
c = children (3-10 yrs); t = teenagers (11-20 yrs);
w = women (21-59 yrs); m = men (21-64 yrs);
wp = women pensioners (60 + yrs); mp = men pensioners (65 + yrs)
* includes small proportion in two car households

The pattern of children's journeys on foot reflects the three categories of households without a car, with one car, and with at least two cars. The first household car reduces the extent of walking as it enables more journeys to be made, particularly at weekends, to destinations that cannot be reached on foot; a second car in the household leads to this 'service' being available more

Table III.3 Daily journey rates and modal split, by age group and sex, and by access to a car.

	Journeys per person per day: on foot	motorised*	all†	Journeys on foot
	Number			*Per cent*
Children (aged 3—10 years) in households with:				
Two or more cars	0.87	1.68	2.55	34
One car	1.17	1.11	2.28	51
No car	1.36	0.46	1.82	75
All children aged 3—10 years	1.18	1.01	2.19	54
Women pensioners (60 years and over):				
Two or more cars	0.56	1.19	1.75	32
One car	0.72	1.07	1.79	40
No car	0.76	0.64	1.40	54
All women pensioners	0.74	0.78	1.52	49
Men pensioners (65 years and over):				
Two or more cars	0.44	1.78	2.22	20
One car, with licence	0.60	1.82	2.42	25
One car, no licence	0.56	0.55	1.11	50
No car	0.97	0.95	1.62	60
All men pensioners	0.82	1.01	1.83	45
Teenagers (aged 11—20 years) in households with:				
Two or more cars	0.76	2.23	2.99	25
One car	1.25	1.62	2.87	43
No car	1.20	1.24	2.44	49
All teenagers aged 11—20 years	1.14	1.61	2.75	41
Women (aged 21—59 years):				
Two or more cars, with licence	0.46	2.75	3.21	14
Two or more cars, no licence	0.77	1.62	2.39	32
One car, with licence	0.85	2.30	3.15	27
One car, no licence	1.09	1.44	2.53	43
No car	1.24	1.04	2.28	54
All women aged 21—59 years	0.98	1.71	2.69	36
Men (aged 21—64 years):				
Two or more cars	0.41	2.48	2.89	14
One car, with licence	0.46	2.71	3.17	15
One car, no licence	0.93	1.44	2.37	39
No car, with licence	0.96	1.54	2.50	38
No car, no licence	1.08	1.29	2.37	46
All men aged 21—64 years	0.62	2.28	2.90	21

*Includes cycling.

†Excludes journeys made in the course of work.

often, especially for taking children to school rather than them going on foot. The effect on walking of car availability is reflected in the fact that only one third of the journeys of children in households with two or more cars are made on foot; in contrast, the proportions are a half in one car households and three quarters in no car households.

On the other hand, there is less difference among teenagers in households with no car and one car; under one half of their journeys are made on foot, suggesting that parents are less willing to chauffeur them once they can act responsibly in dangerous traffic, or alternatively, that the attractions of car travel are not sufficient compensation for the likely loss of independence when travelling with parents. However, there is a marked decline in walking when the household has two or more cars and the teenager is more likely to have optional use of the second car. Indeed, over half of those eligible to take the driving test in these households have passed it; as a result only a quarter of the journeys of the teenagers in two car households are made on foot.

The pattern of walking for men of working age with licences in both one and two car households is very similar because in either instance licence holding is generally synonomous with having a car at their disposal; for women, such motorised mobility is far more likely to necessitate membership of a two car household. Thus the pattern of walking of women licence holders in two car households is very similar to that of men in one or two car households, that is, there is little reliance on walking. In one car households women rely more heavily on walking though, if they can drive, they do sometimes have individual use of the car so they make more journeys generally than those who cannot drive, but make fewer of them on foot. On the other hand, women (and the few men) who live in car owning households but who cannot drive have more in common with adults in households without a car: that is an increased reliance on walking but a lower activity rate overall. Pensioners, too, have a lower activity rate overall though not always as regards walking, for each type of pensioner relies on walking somewhat more than his or her younger counterpart.

Figure 3.2 also illustrates graphically what a distorted view of daily travel is obtained if walking is ignored and if, as happens in many planning and transport planning exercises, attention is concentrated primarily on the motorised journey to work.

Distance walked

It was noted in Chapter II that just under three quarters of all journeys on foot are less than one mile long. Surprisingly, this proportion varies only slightly with household car ownership, but it does vary with age and by car ownership within age group. Children's journeys on foot are particularly self-contained reflecting the proximity of primary schools, and perhaps parental constraints on the geographical range of their activity. In fact, the median walk for children is only 75 per cent of that for men of working age and 70 per cent of that for teenagers.

The relatively high incidence of short journeys on foot among women of

Table III.4 Journeys on foot, according to distance, age group, and sex

| | Journeys on foot*: | | | Median journey distance (yards) |
	Less than half a mile	Half a mile but less than 1 mile	1 mile and over	
	Per cent			
Children aged 3—10 years	50	30	20	885
Teenagers aged 11—20 years	39	27	35	1,258
Men aged 21—64 years	40	28	32	1,188
Women aged 21—59 years	44	29	26	1,047
Men pensioners, 65 years and over	34	30	36	1,348
Women pensioners, 60 years and over	41	33	26	1,109
All groups	43	29	28	1,100

*Excluding the walking at either end of many motorised journeys.

working age also indicates the local nature of their daily lives, whilst among women pensioners a further contributory factor is likely to be the difficulty that many of them have in walking very far. The availability of concessionary fares might encourage some to make more use of buses; pensioners with such concessions walk slightly shorter distances than those without. The median length of men pensioners' walks is the longest for all groups reflecting the fact that they are prepared or able to walk for a longer time without difficulty. Men of working age, too, if they have no car, make a relatively high proportion of long walk journeys, especially for essential purposes. These are probably their journeys to work, pointing yet again to the bias in a transport planning system which concentrates attention on the motorised journey to work and pays little heed to the problems of people who walk — for these working age men without cars tend to be among the lower paid and less skilled sections of society.

Income and Socio-economic Group

Household income and socio-economic group (SEG) are, in fact, closely associated with car ownership[5]: Table III.5 shows how much more people in low income and 'blue collar' households rely on walking, in terms of the proportion of their journeys made on foot. This enhanced significance for walking does not result from a much greater number of walk journeys, however, but from a smaller number of motorised journeys—the bus does not fulfil the same function for them as a car does for others.

Further analysis shows that this variation does not result directly from the influence of income or SEG themselves, but from their influence on car ownership. In fact, 'white collar' non-car owners tend to make more walk

[5] Appendix C shows the variation in car ownership according to household income and socio-economic group.

Table III.5 Daily journey rates and modal split, by household income and socio-economic group of head of household

	Journeys per person per day: on foot	motorised	all methods	Journeys on foot
Gross household income				
	Number			*Per cent*
£10,000 p.a. and over	0.71	2.68	3.39	21
£9,999-7,500 p.a.	0.73	2.34	3.07	24
£7,499-5,000 p.a.	0.87	2.06	2.93	30
£4,999-3,000 p.a.	0.92	1.88	2.70	34
£2,999-1,500 p.a.	0.98	1.36	2.34	42
Under £1,500 p.a.	0.86	0.84	1.70	51
Socio-economic group of head of household*				
white collar 1	0.82	2.39	3.21	26
2	0.77	2.08	2.85	27
3	0.97	1.85	2.82	34
blue collar 4	0.93	1.61	2.54	37
5	0.94	1.41	2.35	40
6	0.94	1.15	2.09	45

*For definitions of socio-economic group, see Appendix A, para 16

journeys but fewer journeys overall when compared with people in 'blue collar' households who do own cars. Similarly, high income non-car owners tend to make more walk journeys but fewer journeys overall when compared with lower income car owners. Overriding this, of course, is the fact that on the whole low income and 'blue collar' households are far less likely to have a car, giving the overall results shown in the table. Moreover, examination of distances walked shows that, apart from women pensioners, poorer people—particularly in households without a car—are somewhat more likely to walk longer distances; this suggests that they are doing so to economise on the costs of motorised travel where this is feasible.

Bus Service

By using other NTS data it can be shown that the quality of the bus service in terms of its frequency influences very slightly the pattern of walking—and certainly much less so than the changes associated with the availability of a household car. Where services are less frequent, the proportion of journeys on foot is not affected, though the average distance walked increases slightly because it is then probably more practical to walk to relatively distant destinations than to wait for a bus.

This variation in distance walked is not marked, however, because of the fairly close association of two influential but contradictory factors: poorer bus services, which discourage bus use, tend to be in the same areas as less accessible facilities, which have the effect of encouraging bus use. Nevertheless, better services also affect travel patterns more generally, for where services are more frequent, there is a transfer of a roughly equivalent number of journeys to bus from car lifts as from walking.

Comparison of 1972/73 and 1975/76

Chapter II showed that people reported about 20 per cent fewer journeys on foot in 1975/76 compared with 1972/73. It can also be seen from the NTS that the change occurs equivalently among people in households with two, one or no cars. Table III.6 shows this to be so, though the *absolute* change is highest for those originally walking most—that is the non-car owners. In no type of household does the change imply an increase in motorised travel; instead it leads to a drop in the total number of journeys by all modes recorded in the survey. This amounts to a reduction of about one in eight journeys, and because of their initially greater reliance on walking and smaller decline in motorised travel, the reduced walk activity of non-car owners accounts for virtually all the decline by all forms of travel.

Table III.6   Daily journey rates and model split, by household car ownership, 1972/73 and 1975/76

	Journeys per person per day:						Change in walk journeys as per cent of all 1972/73 journeys
	on foot			all methods			
	1972/73	1975/76	Per cent change	1972/73	1975/76	Per cent change	
Number of cars in household:							
Two or more	0.76	0.60	− 21	3.46	3.05	− 12	− 5
One	1.13	0.88	− 22	3.22	2.83	− 12	− 7
None	1.32	1.07	− 20	2.30	2.01	− 13	− 12

The proportional decline in walking was highest for women and children[6] and least for men pensioners, with part of these changes reflecting the difference in car ownership between the two surveys, which in turn partly reflects the differences in areas sampled. When car ownership is controlled, there emerges no consistent pattern of change for the same type of people in the three types of household, nor even between the two levels of car ownership. The reduction in walking varies widely, from a decline of 33 per

---

[6] Women (aged 21-59) − 25%; children (aged 3-10) − 24%; women (aged 60 or over) − 22%; men (aged 21-64) − 19%; teenagers (aged 11-20) − 19%; men (aged 65 and over) − 13%.

cent among women (aged 21-59) in two car households, to only one per cent for non-car owning men pensioners (who as seen earlier tend to report longer than average walk journeys). Some of the changes, and the journey purposes related to them, are discussed in more detail in later sections.

Pedestrians at Risk in Road Accidents

In addition to the association with pedestrian travel, personal characteristics can be examined in relation to their association with pedestrian casualties. As is fairly well known, young people are the most vulnerable pedestrians: children up to the age of 14 account for 42 per cent of pedestrian casualties but only 24 per cent of the population. In one respect this is not too surprising, for it will be recalled children also make most of their journeys on foot—accounting for 31 per cent of all pedestrian journeys. However, as Table III.7 shows, by relating the annual figures for road accidents to the average number of journeys that people in each age group make on foot each day, young children's journeys are the most hazardous. Indeed, their casualty rate per journey on foot is nearly three times greater than that for people in their parents' age group. If calculated on a mileage basis, the relative risk to children is even higher for, as noted earlier, their journeys are on average shorter and are less likely to be made on the potentially more dangerous main roads. Pensioners are also more at risk than younger adults, whether the calculation is based on a casualty rate per person or per journey.

Table III.7 Pedestrian casualty rates by age group, 1975/76

Age group	Casualty rate per 100,000 population	
	Per person per day*	Per journey on foot†
5- 9 years	0.88	0.72
10-14 years	0.62	0.48
15-19 years	0.41	0.42
20-29 years	0.22	0.25
30-59 years	0.18	0.23
60-69 years	0.27	0.31
70 years and over	0.40	0.31

*Derived from Department of Transport, *Road Accidents, Great Britain, 1977.*
†Derived from *Road Accidents, Great Britain 1977* and National Travel Survey, 1975/76.

Further analysis of the accident statistics reveals that the pedestrian casualty rate among males is higher than the rate among females. By relating data on the extent of walking to these rates it becomes clear that they are also more prone to accidents when walking: the accident rate among boys is over two thirds higher than among girls even though they walk only slightly more often. As noted earlier in this chapter, men make about one third fewer walk journeys than do women but their pedestrian casualty rate is one third higher.

The number of pedestrian casualities declined by seven per cent between the years 1972/73 and 1975/76. However, it has been seen earlier that the average rate on foot declined even more, indicating that as a travel method walking has become more hazardous than it was previously—in spite of the reduction in the numbers killed and injured.[7] Table III.8 shows that the hazard applied to all age groups, for the journey rates on foot declined more sharply than the accident rate in each group.

Table III.8   Pedestrian casualty rates and number of journeys per person on foot, by age group, 1972/73 and 1975/76

Age group	Casualty rate per 100,000 population		Per cent change in casualty rate	Per cent change in number of journeys per person* 1972/73 and 1975/76
	1972-73†	1975-76†		
5-9 years	418	331	− 21	− 25
10-14 years	272	227	− 17	− 21
15-59 years	94	81	− 14	− 23
60 + years	144	121	− 16	− 18
All	151	126	− 17	− 22

Source: Department of Transport, *Road Accidents, Great Britain, 1977* and National Travel Surveys 1972/73 and 1975/76.
*The age groups for this column are in fact 5-10 years, 11-15 years, 16-59 years and 60 years and over.
† These rates are the average for the two years combined.

This chapter has shown that there are many personal characteristics associated with variations in the frequency with which journeys are made, the proportion of these made on foot, and the distance walked. Access to a car would appear to be the most influential of these characteristics but it must be recalled that this access is itself inextricably linked with other characteristics, influential in their own right and themselves inter-related, including age, sex, income and socio-economic group.

Nevertheless, there are significant groups in the population for whom walking represents a major mode of travel—people in households without a car—including most of those with low incomes, many pensioners, women without a driving licence, children and teenagers. Their relatively high use of walking as a method of getting about in their daily lives effectively defines a much more local catchment of opportunity for their activity. These groups do not appear to spend more time on travelling presumably because of the very fact that much of their activity can still be accomplished within a convenient distance of their home. Clearly, however they can exercise less choice of location for the activity as compared with the more mobile groups in the population. Their greater reliance on walking is also associated with a

---

[7] In fact they have risen since 1976.

42

somewhat lower frequency of activity outside the home. Whether or not this lower quantity of travel could be said to reflect any sort of qualitative deprivation cannot be established from the NTS, which did not include any questions establishing opinions or levels of satisfaction.

It has also been seen in this chapter that the pedestrian casualty rate tends to be higher among those groups more reliant on walking, even when this rate is related to the extent of their walking, and also that walking is becoming more dangerous.

IV Density and Accessibility

One of the basic requirements of pedestrians is to be able to reach the people or places they need or wish to visit. In view of the distance which can conveniently be covered on foot, access by walking implies proximity and the NTS in 1975/76 provided, for the first time, national information on this with data about the proximity of some basic facilities. The information gives some indication first of the 'self sufficiency' of different types of areas in respect of these facilities, and second of the access, for different people, to a range of facilities commonly used in daily life. The facilities are grocers' shops, post offices, chemists, doctors' surgeries, chain stores and hospitals, the last two representing less frequently used facilities.

The accessibility of facilities is related to their size, or scale, and the population density of the areas in which they are located. In theory, the density of each area determines how many people live within a certain distance of a facility and so, if a number of areas have differing population densities but a certain type of facility is provided at a uniform scale (each one serving the same number of people), then the access in the different areas will vary, in a manner directly proportional to the density of the area. If the scale of a facility increases rather than remaining uniform, while density decreases, the variation in access will be sharper; if on the other hand the scale of a facility increases *with* density, then the accessibility will tend to equalise.[1] In other words, equal access between areas would result from having lots of small scale facilities in low density areas and fewer, but larger scale facilities in high density areas. In any one area, of course, access will vary between facilities which are basically neighbourhood or district in character, and those which serve a wider area.

In practice, the NTS shows that some significant variations in access do occur within, as well as between, different types of facility, as revealed in Figure 4.1. Substantial and so impractical or uneconomic adjustments to the scale and number of facilities would therefore be required to equalise access for all areas and for any one type of facility. More realistically, the NTS data can show whether and what sort of area is likely to fall below a given standard

---

[1] If changes in scale are gradual between areas, the gradient will be smooth; if changes in scale are abrupt the gradient will be 'stepped' and inequalities in access more noticeable.

Figure 4.1 Access to facilities and household car ownership, by population density

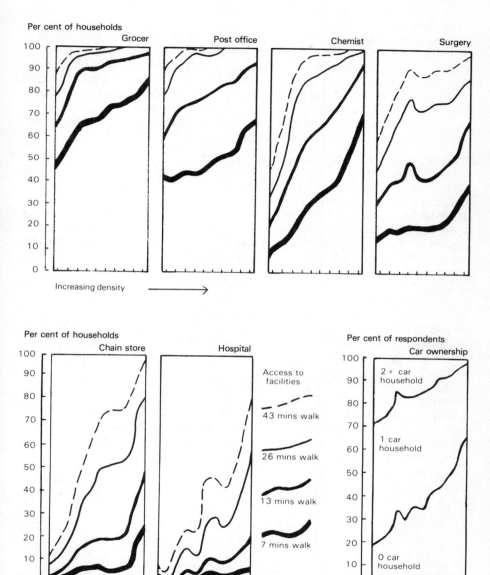

For definitions of density, see Appendix "A"

of access for a particular facility, for instance a five minute walk to a grocer or a ten minute walk to a doctor's surgery.

These considerations of access, scale and density need to be taken into account when opportunities arise to review planning options, for it is worth emphasising that options which increase the capacity of existing facilities, or which provide large scale new facilities, have the effect of extending catchment areas. As the previous discussion indicates, this effect is exaggerated if the population served or even part of it, lives in areas of low residential density; such options can thus create lengthy journeys and thereby cause inconvenience or even hardship for some of the intended users. Location is also relevant; a facility sited at the periphery of its service area is naturally easily accessible to fewer people than one which is centrally located.

Density, Access and Car Ownership

On average, 70 per cent of households in the NTS have a shop within easy access, that is, about a five minute walk or less from home. Figure 4.1 illustrates that this average hides a range from one half of the households in areas of lowest population density to over four fifths of households in the areas of highest density.[2] The decline in access is fairly gradual, as it is with the slightly more distant post offices and chemists. Surgeries are more equitably distributed by area, but with a lower average level of access; over half the households are at least a quarter of an hour's walk from one.

The NTS also allows the relationship between car ownership and density to be explored. Thus while Figure 4.1 shows polarisation between people in high and low density areas in terms of their access to facilities, it also shows a similar differentiation by car ownership. In the highest density areas this is only half the level found in the lowest density areas; the ownership of two cars shows an equivalent variation, with a particularly smooth grading between the extremes.[3]

When the findings for car ownership and access are viewed together, some strong similarities emerge. It is commonly accepted that considerations of access in general (including the lack of access to adequate levels of public transport) account for much of the high level of car ownership in rural areas compared with large cities. What is not so well known is the similarity across a much wider range of areas between the rate of decline in car ownership and the rate of increase in access to four very commonly used facilities.[4] This is clearly shown in Figure 4.1; it also shows that the rate of increase in the ownership of two cars is similar to the rate at which 'poor' access on foot to these facilities (a walk of half an hour or more) varies by density.[5]

---

[2] For definition of density, see Appendix A, para 17.

[3] The NTS 1972/73 contained similar findings, though on the basis of slightly lower levels of car ownership overall. The middle densities showed the largest increases between 1972/73 and 1975/76.

[4] When access is defined as easily accessible on foot and so involving only a five or ten minute walk.

[5] This does not hold true for access to chain stores and hospitals—but then these are not generally considered to be 'local' facilities, and so variations in walk access would not be expected to influence car ownership; the public transport service is probably more influential in these instances.

Table IV.1 Variation in car ownership by population density, within income groups*

	Population density										
	(lowest)							(highest)			All density bands
	1	2	3	4	5	6	7	8	9	10	
	Per cent										
High income											
Households with no car	5	8	11	12	10	12	18	16	19	29	14
Households with 2 or more cars	43	31	29	36	32	22	25	30	15	7	28
Medium-high income											
Households with no car	15	21	23	20	27	31	31	36	39	56	29
Households with 2 or more cars	17	12	8	7	8	7	6	3	4	2	8
Low-medium income											
Households with no car	31	45	50	52	52	64	59	66	70	80	56
Low income											
Households with no car	82	82	86	87	90	90	94	95	94	97	90

*The high income group is defined as those earning £5,000 p.a. or more; medium-high income group are those with incomes between £3,000 and £5,000 p.a. The low-medium group covers those with incomes in the range £1,500 to £3,000 p.a. while the low income group is defined as those receiving under £1,500 p.a.

It could be argued that the variation in car ownership is not a reflection of physical or planning characteristics, but the result of differences in the social, economic and age profiles of different areas, these variables being closely associated with levels of car ownership. But the NTS shows that although there are variations in the social profiles of different areas, these are far less significant than the variations in car ownership within equivalent income or social groups; thus the same income group reports considerably different levels of car ownership according to where they live.[6] Tables IV.1, IV.2, and IV.3 indicate this elasticity in car ownership, showing a substantial swing into car ownership among 'blue collar', low income or elderly groups in low density areas and an equivalent swing away from it among 'white collar' or high income groups in high density areas. Thus, the variation in car ownership within groups, according to where they live means that though the proportion of households with low incomes ranges from 23 per cent (in low density areas) to 34 per cent (in high density areas), the proportion of all households without a car ranges much more widely—from 20 per cent to 60 per cent.

[6] The only major difference by density is a switch within the 'white collar' group, with managerial and professional occupations dominating in the low densities and intermediate 'white collar' in the high. This somewhat, but by no means wholly, explains the difference in two-car ownership by area. Low and high density areas have similar proportions of high income households and pensioner households.

Table IV.2 Variation in car ownership by population density, within socio-economic group

| | Population density | | | | | | | | | | All density bands |
| | (lowest) | | | | | | | (highest) | | | |
	1	2	3	4	5	6	7	8	9	10	
					Per cent						
Professional/managerial											
Households with no car	7	8	9	11	10	14	13	19	24	32	13
Households with 2 or more cars	37	37	32	31	36	29	24	26	18	9	30
Other white collar											
Households with no car	18	26	28	31	42	35	41	44	52	70	40
Skilled manual											
Households with no car	21	23	38	35	36	42	45	45	46	54	39
Semi-skilled manual											
Households with no car	50	55	55	56	69	60	67	66	74	80	63
Unskilled manual											
Households with no car	60	74	78	83	85	83	86	84	87	95	82

The reasons for these large differences in mobility within groups is no doubt a reflection of a greater need for personal mobility in areas of low accessibility. A further factor to consider is that not only are these areas less likely to have local facilities of various kinds, but access to these or other facilities at more distant locations is also difficult by public transport. Indeed, in the lowest density areas, 10 per cent of households reported that they did not have a daily bus service and almost a further 50 per cent have a very infrequent bus service (a small number of buses a day); in the second lowest density area, over one third have a service as poor as this. By contrast, over two thirds of households in the two highest density areas have bus services which provide a better than half-hourly service.

Table IV.3 Variation in pensioner's car ownership and female licence holding, by population density

| | Population density | | | | | | | | | | All density bands |
| | (lowest) | | | | | | | (highest) | | | |
	1	2	3	4	5	6	7	8	9	10	
					Per cent						
Pensioners in car-owning household	51	46	38	33	31	33	31	26	21	12	31
Women with driving licence	45	37	26	34	34	29	23	22	20	18	29

Settlement size

The 1975/76 NTS shows that the size of settlement is related to density, and so to access and car ownership. However, Figure 4.2 illustrates that the relationship with access is rather less consistent in this case, no doubt partly because each urban size contains a range of residential densities. For the larger facilities, too, there may be sudden changes in scale (and thus in access) associated with particular population thresholds. For car ownership, it is the relatively high ownership in Greater London which creates the inconsistency, perhaps reflecting the higher income levels there compared with the northern conurbations.[7]

Figure 4.2   Access to facilities and household car ownership, by settlement size

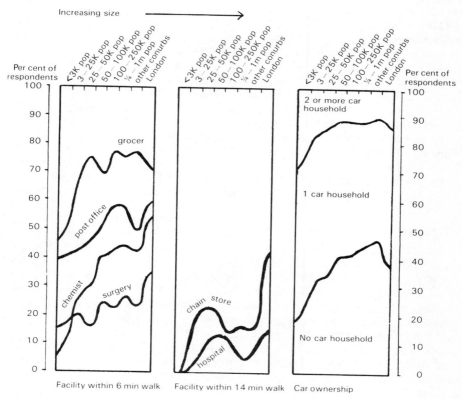

Facility within 6 min walk   Facility within 14 min walk   Car ownership

---

[7]The 1972/73 NTS included higher levels of car ownership in the conurbations and large towns, but significantly lower levels in towns of under 50,000 population and in rural areas, when compared with the 1975/76 survey.

49

Density and the Pattern of Walking

In view of the relationships described earlier, it is not surprising to find that, as density increases, there is a steady rise in the proportion of journeys made on foot together with a slight increase in the number of these journeys. At the same time, both the proportion and the number of motorised journeys decline.

The change in walking patterns is almost wholly related to travel on essential journeys as Table IV.4 shows; this reflects the better access to facilities enjoyed in higher density areas and the lower levels of car ownership there. Much less is known about access to the type of facility or place visited on optional journeys, but for these there is only a slight variation in the amount of walking in the different areas. However, it is significant that activity which is optional does not decline in the higher density areas, in spite of the greater number of people without cars and the fact that non-car owners on the whole make fewer optional journeys than car owners.[8]

Overall, the proportion of journeys on foot jumps from 27 per cent in low density areas to 45 per cent in the highest density areas, reflecting the increase in opportunities within walking distance. For some journey purposes, though, the general trend is reversed in the areas of highest density—not for the proportion of journeys on foot (which continues to increase) but for their number (which drops for both optional and essential journeys). What appears to be happening is a slight but significant switch from walking to public transport, though walking remains the more common method of the two. This trend can also be seen in most of the conurbation areas. The use of public transport does, in fact, increase across all densities at the expense of car travel. And with walking also taking the place of further car travel, the fall in the use of the car is substantial; in the top density band car travel is less common than either walking or public transport, and walking takes precedence over car travel in the top three bands.

Length of Journeys on Foot

The distribution of journeys on foot by length is surprisingly similar in all areas: Table IV.5 shows that there are more short journeys in areas of higher density, but that the number and proportion of long ones also increases.[9] The average length is, if anything, slightly longer in areas of higher density. These findings are surprising in view of the better local access in these areas, which would be expected to encourage short walks, and the fact that these areas have better public transport, which would be expected to 'absorb' some of the long walks. The explanation is likely to be that although high density does mean that some facilities are accessible within a short walk from home, it may also mean more choice and better facilities being available within the catchment of a somewhat longer walk. In other words, those areas give a better return for the investment of the extra time and effort involved — especially as the higher

---

[8] See Chapter III.
[9] A short journey is defined as under ½ mile; a medium journey as ½ mile but under 1 mile, and a long journey as one of 1 mile or over.

Table IV.4 Variation in walking, by population density

	Population density									
	(lowest)									(highest)
	1	2	3	4	5	6	7	8	9	10
	Per cent of journeys on foot									
All purposes	27	29	38	33	34	36	37	39	41	45
All essential journeys:	26	28	36	34	36	38	38	41	44	46
education	39	38	54	53	66	68	64	69	74	64
shopping	32	38	44	43	44	45	48	50	54	66
personal business	28	34	44	34	36	33	40	36	46	56
escort	16	24	31	25	21	23	31	45	42	36
work	16	14	20	20	17	22	22	19	22	21
All optional journeys	30	35	40	36	36	36	35	37	34	40
recreation	64	75	65	63	62	62	68	61	58	71
social	12	25	25	18	144	22	25	28	25	30
	No. of journeys per 100 people per day									
All journeys*										
all methods	244	254	244	272	261	261	258	266	258	220
on foot	66	73	91	90	89	94	94	103	105	98
Essential journeys:										
all methods	152	166	161	176	171	171	169	175	175	153
on foot	40	46	59	59	61	64	65	72	77	70
Optional journeys:										
all methods	79	76	80	85	79	81	80	82	76	67
on foot	24	26	31	30	28	29	28	30	26	27

*Includes essential and optional journeys and also those made in the course of work (not included in essential *personal* travel) and those not classified by purpose.

densities are found closer to the hearts of cities, where there are many sizes and types of facility. As for the availability of public transport, it would appear from the table that the area of topmost density can in fact offer a service which is convenient enough to cause a transfer from the longer walks. Thus there is, in general, a slight lengthening in the average walk journey as density increases, but this trend is halted and then just reversed in the top two density bands. As already noted, however, such areal variations are very small.

Variation by car ownership

The proportion of journeys made on foot in areas of different density does not simply reflect the variation in car ownership. This, of course, has a bearing on the amount of walking, but the changing balance between travel methods is not a straighforward substitution of walking by one type of person in place of

51

Table IV.5   Length of walk journeys, by population density

Distance	Population density									
	(lowest)									(highest)
	1	2	3	4	5	6	7	8	9	10
	Number of walk journeys per 100 people per day									
Less than ½ mile	31	32	41	34	39	38	37	41	44	41
1 mile and over	14	20	25	26	25	25	28	32	31	25
	Per cent of walk journeys									
Less than ½ mile	13	13	17	13	15	15	15	15	17	18
1 mile and over	22	28	28	29	28	27	31	31	30	26

car travel by a different type of person. In the first instance, over three-quarters of car journeys are two miles or more in length, distances which the non-car owner is unlikely to walk. The substitution of walking does occur, however, indicating not only that the travel method changes but also the distance travelled. Secondly, it is probable that some people in the lower density areas do not use their nearest facility, which they may be able to reach on foot, but choose to go further afield, by car. The question then arises as to why their higher density counterparts are not also acquiring cars and exercising similar choice — for as seen earlier many high density non-car owners are the same type of people as lower density car owners. In these instances the difference in travel between areas results not only from a substitution in travel method, nor only from the choice of destination, but also from a substitution in mobility; in other words, where a non-car owner in a high density area will walk, a similar person in a low density area is more likely to become a car owner—and then use his car.

Some of the influence bringing about these varying patterns of behaviour no doubt stems from the difficulty of using cars in some areas; but it is also probable that part of it results from variations in the patterns of land use and the location of facilities. These factors mean that there is less need to acquire or use cars in areas of higher density, because of the greater potential for local travel, combined with an improved level of public transport for longer journeys. Thus, as Table IV.6 shows, with increasing density, people in car owning households make more and more of their essential journeys on foot; though on optional journeys the greater choice of destination open to car users appears to be more influential. The same is not true of people in non-car owning households; they have a high level of walking for both optional and essential journeys in low and high density areas alike. Unlike people with cars, they cannot as easily opt for motorised travel in low density areas, for the bus services are poor. Local access is poor, too, but the lack of local facilities in low density areas leads to a smaller number of people being without cars, as noted earlier, rather than the non-car owners making only a small proportion of their journeys on foot.

Table IV.6   Variation in walking, by car ownership and population density

	Population density									
	(lowest)									(highest)
	1	2	3	4	5	6	7	8	9	10
	Per cent of journeys on foot									
Two car or more households:										
essential journeys	14	16	25	18	16	28	22	22	30	40
optional journeys	20	19	23	18	21	25	24	23	15	25
One car households:										
essential journeys	27	28	32	29	33	34	32	36	39	38
optional journeys	28	36	37	30	32	31	29	31	30	26
No car households:										
essential journeys	46	49	56	56	55	55	56	55	55	54
optional journeys	56	50	58	58	52	55	52	50	45	55
Per cent of people in household without a car, in each area	21	24	34	31	35	34	41	44	50	60

Moreover, though the lower density areas have low levels of accessibility, they do contain some facilities, and households living close to these facilities tend to include somewhat higher levels of non-car owners than is normal for these areas, as Table IV.7 shows. Non-car owners in these areas, therefore, tend to have higher levels of access than is general for low density areas. At the other end of the spectrum, non-car owners who live in the higher density areas have access to relatively good bus services and through these to a greater choice of facilities, as well as having more facilities available locally. A final factor affecting the level of walking in different areas is that non-car owners in the higher density areas tend to include a slightly higher number of employed people[10], so that the distribution of journeys will include more travel to and from work — a journey which tends to involve longer distance travel requiring use of the bus or train (or underground in London).

Variation by age

The relationship between walking and density is heightened for men and women below pensionable age, because in areas of low density and access they are increasingly likely to have a car available through the ownership of one or two cars and the possession of a driving licence. This is particularly so for men, who show the biggest shift towards walking in high density areas: their walk journeys double. Even so, in each type of area they are the least common group to be found as pedestrians.

Teenagers, too, benefit from increased car ownership in areas of low density; they or their friends may be able to drive or a parent may be willing to

[10] In urban areas stage buses are mostly used; in rural areas most of these journeys are on 'other public transport'—generally special buses provided at no cost to pupils.

Table IV.7 Variation in non-car ownership according to the access to facilities in areas of low population density

| | Population density | | |
	Lowest density areas	Second lowest density areas	Third lowest density areas
	Per cent of households with no car		
Walk time to shopping facilities:			
Less than 6 minutes	31	31	43
14 or more minutes	20	21	31
Walk time to post office:			
Less than 6 minutes	28	27	41
14 or more minutes	24	27	34
All households	27	28	39

offer a lift. They also benefit from public transport in the higher density areas, however, and are perhaps more disposed or able to use it in comparison with their parents or younger siblings. Their walk patterns thus do not show as significant a variation by density.

Children's travel varies far more, with a strong and consistent increase in walking as density rises. The number of journeys made on foot increases from 90 in the lowest density areas to 135 per day per 100 children in the highest, accounting for less than 40 per cent to over 70 per cent of their journeys. This applies mainly to their essential journeys reflecting the distance travelled to school. In contrast to their fathers they are among the most common pedestrians in each type of area.

Pensioners are more dependent on public transport than most people, and its availability — and the wider availability of concessionary fares — appears to offset slightly the influence of access in areas of higher density. However, they are also likely to encounter difficulties in walking, with the result that they make fewer journeys on foot or by motorised means in the lower density areas which tend both to lack good public transport and concessionary fares and to have low walk accessibility.

This chapter has looked at the broad variations in travel according to density, within the context of the variations that also occur in accessibility and car ownership. In the chapters that follow the travel patterns associated with specific journey purposes and population groups are examined in more detail and the influence of area is assessed.

V School Journeys

The journey to and from school involves children and teenagers in their most frequent travel purpose, accounting for about 40 per cent of all their journeys. Schools are traditionally viewed as community facilities and most of the travel associated with them is on foot; 60 per cent of all school journeys, (including those for further and higher education) are made in this way. In spite of this, or perhaps because it is so commonly understood, public discussion about school provision does not always entail reference to guidelines on travel and accessibility, though road safety does feature as a matter of public concern. Attention does not usually centre on the desirability of needing motorised transport to school either, but on whether it is needed, and the criteria for determining this. Attention focuses on the management and cost of providing transport for those pupils who live 'beyond reasonable walking distance' from their nearest suitable school. These distances were regarded in the 1944 Education Act as being two miles for children up to eight years old and three miles for those children over eight, in each direction, though a Department of Education and Science (DES) Working Party in 1973 concluded that these distances exceed what is now considered to be acceptable. The Working Party also suggested that distance should not be the sole nor even the main criterion for determining the availability of school transport, and that safety even over short distances should be taken into account.[1]

However, for most pupils the nearest suitable school lies well within these limits and it is, in any case, general policy to provide smaller more local infant and junior schools compared with secondary schools. In 1976 the average primary school had about 220 pupils while the average secondary school had nearly four times this number — about 830 — and the associated travel patterns reflect this. It is therefore appropriate to look at the school journeys to primary and secondary school separately.

Primary School

Children's journeys to and from primary schools account for the highest level of walking found in the NTS — over seven in ten of them are made on

---

[1] Department of Education and Science, *School Transport, Report of the Working Party, 1973.*

foot, which is more than double the average for all personal travel. The proportion of children who walk is somewhat lower than this, because returning home at lunchtime is more common among those who walk to school and live close to it. These children thus make four walk journeys each day, whereas others who travel by bus or even car are more likely to make just two journeys each day. This does not, however, reduce the overall supremacy of walking. When lunch time journeys are excluded and just morning and afternoon travel is considered, walking is still seen to account for 71 per cent of journeys. At lunchtime, when about one fifth of the primary school children in the NTS returned home, 81 per cent walk.

Seven in ten primary school journeys are less than one mile long, including 84 per cent of the walk journeys — and half the walk journeys are under half a mile long. Eight in ten of those going home for lunch live within one mile. On the whole the distances walked to school are shorter than for other journey purposes.[2]

The DES Working Party on school transport reported in 1973 that only three per cent of pupils travelled beyond the statutory walking distances. Free transport was not necessarily provided for these, if their long distance travel was by choice rather than necessity; on the other hand, some authorities provided free transport for children travelling less than the statutory distance. These two items in fact cancelled each other out with the result that three per cent of all children did receive free transport: nine per cent travelled between one mile and the two or three mile limit unaided and nine per cent travelled over the limit unaided.

Children's essential travel, of which school journeys comprise 60 per cent, is more strongly associated with density and type of area than is the travel of any other group. Walking rises sharply with density, reflecting increasingly smaller areas of school catchment and so shorter journeys. It may also be true that schools in older, high density urban areas are smaller in roll size, and so even smaller in catchment, than their more modern counterparts in newer, lower density urban housing areas.

There is substantially more walking in urban than in rural areas — in the latter, walking accounts for only 57 per cent of children's school journeys but in the former, for 76 per cent. Nearly all the remaining journeys are divided between cars and public transport: in urban areas the ratio is 2:1 but in rural areas it is 3:2, representing relatively more public transport use (including, of course, special school buses) in spite of higher car ownership. Cycling is very rare, especially in urban areas.[3] If village children do walk to school, the distance is likely to be slightly shorter than in urban areas; on the other hand the average distance travelled by all travel methods is greater.

---

[2] There is no information in the NTS about the accessibility of primary schools, but in an earlier PEP survey in part of South East England, 80 per cent of the mothers of young children reported having a primary school within a ten minute walk of their home. See M. Hillman *et al, Transport Realities and Planning Policy,* op. cit.

[3] Three per cent of all journeys in rural areas were reported to have taken place by bicycle. The equivalent figure for towns was one per cent; none was recorded in metropolitan areas.

Though children have less use of household cars than their parents, that use is significant enough to result in much less walking to school among children in two car households; under half of them walk, in contrast to three quarters of those with one car and seven in eight of those without a car. Rather surprisingly, those with two cars do not walk the shortest distances but the longest — one quarter of their walk journeys are over one mile long, whereas only one in eight of non-car owners' walk journeys are this length. It may be that those in car owning, and especially two car owning households live in areas with relatively poor access to schools, or possibly that their parents exercise more choice, selecting a school which is not the nearest. Also, because some children in car owning households travel to and from school by different methods[4] it may be that some of the longer walks are by children who are given a lift in the morning but who walk home in the afternoon. The NTS shows, in fact, that walking is more common and car travel less common in the afternoon compared with the morning; and the additional afternoon walk journeys are longer than average.

Children whose school journeys are made by car are not the only ones who are escorted on the journey. The NTS shows that over half the escorted journeys to school are on foot, and as some of the motorised escorted journeys are to secondary school, then well over half the escorted primary school journeys must be on foot, reflecting parents' concern over traffic danger on the journey. Chapter II showed this concern to be well founded. In fact, one third of the annual 33,000 or so child pedestrian casualties occur on Mondays to Fridays between the hours of 8 and 9 am or 3 and 5 pm.

Several studies have provided information on the safety aspect of the school journey. PEP surveys have examined adult accompaniment and related this broadly to traffic levels and dangers; other studies have related travel to the number and nature of hazards *en route* and to the relationship between distance and road crossing; and others have studied children's perceptions of road signs and their road crossing behaviour.[5] As noted earlier, recognition of the vulnerability of children to traffic has led to various measures being taken to reduce the annual toll of death and injury attributable to this cause — local authority road safety officers and the police visit schools regularly, 'lollipop' men and women are employed to take children across busy roads near schools, guard rails are installed and school warning signs displayed to alert motorists, road humps are being tested and road width restrictions imposed to slow down traffic more forcibly near schools, and publicity campaigns are aimed at impressing the need for caution on parents, children and motorists alike.

There is evidence, though, of other developments affecting school journeys which are likely to counter these efforts as they will mean that longer walk

[4] M. Hillman et al., *Transport realities and planning policy*, op. cit.
[5] For example P. H. Levin and A. J. Bruce, *The Location of Primary Schools*, Building Research Station (1968). M. Hillman et al., *Personal mobility and transport policy*, op. cit.; and *Transport realities and planning policy*, op. cit.; Helen V. Colborne, *Two experiments on training children in road safety*, Transport and Road Research Laboratory, LR404, (1971); T. S. M. Jones, *Young children and their school journey*, Transport and Road Research Laboratory, SR 342, (1977).

journeys will have to be made which will therefore increase children's exposure to traffic. At the same time, however, the number of children walking to school is declining.

Comparison of 1972/73 and 1975/76

Insofar as travel patterns reflect accessibility, the 1975/76 NTS indicates a generally good level of access to primary schools, but a comparison with the 1972/73 findings prompts questions about changes in access and about what are desirable patterns of access and travel for the future. Table V.1 shows a reduction in walking in all areas and a lengthening of distances walked between the two surveys. Changes in the rural areas are particularly dramatic; whilst these areas had hardly any long walks to primary school recorded in 1972/73, by 1975/76 almost one in every eleven journeys, by all methods, were long walks. Even in the urban areas very short walks (under half a mile) dropped from almost 50 per cent of *all* primary school journeys to under 40 per cent.

Table V.1 **Walking to primary school* in different areas, 1972/73 and 1975/76**

	NTS	Journeys on foot	Walk journeys in miles:		
			Less than ½ mile	½ but less than 1 mile	1 mile or more
		Per cent	*Per cent*		
All areas	72/73	79	59	31	10
	75/76	73	51	33	16
Metropolitan areas	72/73	80	56	34	9
	75/76	77	47	37	16
Other urban areas	72/73	81	59	30	12
	75/76	76	53	31	17
Rural areas	72/73	61	70	29	1
	75/76	57	55	30	15

*This table records the education journeys of children aged 5—10 years.

No doubt some of the decline in walking has resulted from the rise in car ownership between the two surveys and from more mothers being able to drive and having access to the household's car or second car where one exists. In these circumstances, a choice can then be made to drive children to school which would thereby have been recorded as an increase in car use in the 1975/76 survey at the expense of walking. In fact, the NTS figures do record that the decline in walking is balanced proportionately by increased car use rather than by bus use. But this does not also explain the lengthening of walk journeys; in fact, it would seem more probable that of the mothers acquiring the use of a car, those living further rather than nearer the school would choose to drive there. The effect of this would be to shorten the average walk journey rather than lengthen it. It is likely, therefore, that some of the decline in number and lengthening of distance of walk journeys results from children having to go further to get to school and so being obliged either to walk further or to travel by car or bus. Indeed, there was a reduction in the daily school journey rate (from 135 to 110 per 100 children) which would suggest that fewer children return home at lunchtime (assuming equal numbers of journeys lost through holidays and sickness for each survey). This could be because of the longer walks involved or the need — or the choice — now to use a car or bus. Although bus use as a whole did not increase appreciably there was a shift from ordinary buses to 'other public transport' which includes the special buses paid for by local education authorities for longer distance travel, especially in rural areas.

The nature of the change is, therefore, of shifts from short walks to longer ones, or to longer motorised travel, as well as the straight substitution of travel by car for travel on foot or by stage bus services over the same distance. The change in catchment areas implied by this could result from a number of factors, probably a combination of wider parental choice, school closures, the increase in families living in residential areas with lower standards of access to schools and the rebuilding and relocation of old schools without enough attention being paid to access. Whatever the exact combination, it points to the need for assessments to be made of effects on access and travel when decisions are taken on the location and size of schools, or in discussion about the number of schools required to provide for the educational needs of the population.

A decline in birth rate is seen as usually leading to a decline in the number of schools required — perhaps with redundant schools being put to new uses — though because the children are nevertheless spread over at least as wide an area as before, this means that closure of schools must lead to an increase in the average catchment area of the remaining schools and therefore to longer journeys having to be made. Moreover, closures were occurring even when the school population was increasing fairly substantially during the 1950s and 1960s. Official concern has often been expressed about the age and condition of many school buildings, but not about the declining number of locations and the decline in access concomitant with this. Increases in size have been seen as bestowing educational and financial benefits but the fact that they reduce the overall level of accessibility appears to have been overlooked. Moreover, these benefits need to be weighed against any educational and social consequences (for instance, loss of opportunity to engage in extra-curricular activities after school) which might arise from the loss of independence when children need to be taken to and from school by car or special bus — either because the distance involved requires motorised travel or because the increased walking distance multiplies the traffic hazards en route. Accompaniment may also be necessary if it involves travelling to an unfamiliar neighbourhood, with the

Table V.2 Changes in numbers of primary schools and school roll size 1950—1975

| | Maintained primary schools or departments: | | Middle schools deemed as primary: | |
	Number (000's)	Pupils per school	Number (000's)	Pupils per school
1950	23.1	171	—	—
1955	23.7	194*	—	—
1960	23.4	179	—	—
1965	22.8	187	—	—
1970	23.0	214	0.03	313
1975	22.7	220	0.58	346

Source: DES, *Statistics of Education 1976, Vol. I Schools* (England and Wales) HMSO 1977.
*Period of post-war 'bulge' in numbers of children.

disorientation that this can bring about in a young child.[6]

There are no nationally available data which show precisely the trends in primary school location and access over recent years. Table V.2 shows that there has been a steady decline in the total number of 'schools or departments' since 1955, but the DES does not appear to know how many school sites these cover as the statistics gathered are on an administrative basis and not also on a geographical or locational basis.

For instance, infant and junior departments on the same site but with separate head teachers count as two units, but it is not known whether this practice has become more common nor whether it has tended to replace the provision of two geographically separate primary schools each catering for both infants and juniors. If such developments take place the result is larger catchments without any reduction in the official number of schools. Similarly, if old schools in inner areas of towns are replaced by new ones in new housing areas on the outskirts, then access but not numbers could be affected by a combination of the lower density housing involved and a school location possibly at the edge rather than in the centre of the population catchment it serves. Another example is prompted by the knowledge that changes in travel occurred between 1973 and 1976, for the DES statistics show that the total number of primary schools or departments, including middle schools deemed as primary, did in fact increase slightly in this period, from 23,148 to 23,330.

This increase however, was confined to middle schools; if it was the case that these additional schools were all created by administrative rather than geographical separation, then statistics gathered on a locational basis might have shown an even larger decrease in schools over the period since 1955, leading to larger catchments and longer average journeys.

[6]T. Lee, on the relationship between the school journey and the social and emotional adjustment in rural infant children, *British Journal of Educational Psychology*, Vol. 27, June 1957.

The changes in travel between 1973 and 1976 probably result from a variety of such structural, managerial changes, though it is likely that over a longer period the general trends of school closure and of increased school size shown in Table V.2 have also contributed to travel changes.

School closure is an issue which is causing particular concern in rural areas, where the village school is often seen as an indicator of community viability and where the travel consequences of closure can be particularly drastic. According to a survey conducted in 1977 by *Where* (the Journal of the Advisory Centre for Education) and the Council for the Protection of Rural England (CPRE), there has been an average of one village school closure every week during the last ten years.[7] The survey revealed that Local Education Authorities do consider the travel consequences of closure, many referring to the DES guidelines in force since 1950, which advise a maximum journey time of 45 minutes each way for primary school children. But most authorities view travel time as meaning *motorised* travel time so this maximum could take children many miles from home and much of the concern of local authorities relates to the financial and organisational difficulties of providing special transport. But even if the maximum is related to walking, it implies a distance of about two miles — a long way for young children, especially in a rural area where the settlements are small in scale and where those who live outside the settlements may not have pavements and street lighting as aids to road safety. Yet as the travel data in Table V.1 showed, an increasing number of journeys in these areas take the form of a long walk, possibly indicating an increase in village-to-village or village-to-adjacent-town travel among those not qualifying for special transport.

Comparison of Primary and Secondary School Travel

As noted earlier, secondary schools have larger catchments than primary schools and are less orientated towards particular neighbourhoods. Teenagers' school journeys[8] are therefore not as local — half of them are made on foot rather than three-quarters as is the case with primary school children. For teenagers who do go to school on foot the walks are longer — one third are under half a mile and over one third are at least one mile long, as compared with a half and a sixth respectively for primary school children. Thus as Table V.3 shows, only 33 per cent of all teenagers' school journeys are walks of under one mile in contrast to 61 per cent for children in primary schools. Most non-walk school journeys are at least one mile long.

Secondary School

There is relatively little difference in the travel of teenagers in households with and without a car: 59 per cent and 52 per cent of their respective journeys to school are on foot and, of course, both groups report that just over one third are at least one mile long. In two car households the proportion on foot is

---

[7] Rick Rogers 'Closing Village Schools: what the LEA's are up to', *Where*, 133, Nov./Dec. 1977.

[8] School travel by those aged 11—19 years.

Table V.3 **Modal split and distance walked on travel to primary and secondary school**

Modal split on education journeys	Primary school children		Secondary school children	
	Per cent			
Walking:				
Less than ½ mile	37 ⎫		16 ⎫	
½ mile but less than 1 mile	24 ⎬ 73		17 ⎬ 52	
1 mile or more	12 ⎭		19 ⎭	
Bus/train	7		28	
Car	14		6	
Other	2		7	
N.a.*	4		8	

*See Appendix A, para. 7.

halved, to 28 per cent, but these journeys are somewhat surprisingly longer on average. This finding is similar to the result shown for primary school travel and again could reflect either that two car households are to be found in areas with lower access to facilities or that parents in these households exercise more choice in selecting schools. Moreover, some give their children a lift to school but expect them to walk home in the afternoon, though even in two car households car travel is far less common for school journeys than bus travel. Indeed, public transport, including the subsidised special buses used in many rural areas, is more heavily used in these households than in households without a car.

Parental choice of school, and in some areas the selectivity of schools themselves, could also help to explain the fact that the amount of walking varies between teenagers in 'blue' and 'white collar' households, being lower in the latter. There is also less walking in high rather than low income households. However, in households with no car, the distinctions by socio-economic group and income do not appear. (It should be remembered that lack of a car in 'white collar' and high income households is strongly related to area.)

The variation in walking according to social characteristics is small in relation to the variation that appears on a simple distinction between town and country. This highlights a complete reversal in the balance between walking and public transport[9]; journeys on foot drop from almost 60 per cent in urban areas to 20 per cent in rural areas while use of public transport increases from slightly over 20 per cent to about 60 per cent respectively.[10] Within the urban areas there is somewhat less walking in the metropolitan areas, where the large

---

[9] In the rural areas car travel increases slightly and cycling drops.

[10] In urban areas stage buses are mostly used; in rural areas most of these journeys are on 'other public transport' generally special buses provided at no cost to pupils.

populations support numerous schools, and more extensive public transport networks make them accessible. This compares with a similar trend for teenagers' essential travel as a whole (including work and shopping as well as school journeys) viewed according to density. There is a significant increase in walking between the lowest and the middle density areas (from about a quarter to about a half of essential journeys are made on foot), but the upward trend then ceases, and walking drops suddenly to 40 per cent in the highest density category. The variation is far less extreme and less consistent than for younger children's essential travel which is less oriented to public transport and on which walking increases steadily from 42 per cent of journeys in the lowest to 84 per cent in the highest density areas.

There is a little variation in the length of teenagers' walk journeys to school. The average walk is slightly shorter in rural areas where, if the secondary school is not within easy walking distance, then it is likely to be a considerable distance away and has to be reached by special transport. A wider variation in distance walked on all education travel does appear in relation to the frequency of bus services. There is no difference in the amount of walking, but long walks are more common where the bus services are infrequent and where it is less likely that there is a bus to correspond with the time the school day starts and ends. Although the NTS data do not allow further disaggregation, it would seem that this effect is mainly found in low density areas because special buses are often provided in rural areas.

Table V.4 illustrates teenagers' school travel pattern together with the changes that occurred between the two surveys. As with primary school journeys, those on foot have become longer and there has been a small decrease in their proportion in metropolitan and rural areas.[11]

These findings are surprising for it might have been expected that walking would increase and journeys become shorter during a period which saw a substantial growth in comprehensive education[12] in parallel with reduced attendance at the schools — particularly grammar schools — traditionally associated with extensive catchment areas and thus lengthly or motorised travel.[13] The findings, therefore, must partly reflect the fact that parents can, and do, still exercise considerable choice at the secondary school level. The popularity, reputation and educational standards of schools still vary, and most do not function as 'community schools', although most authorities use proximity as one of the criteria for selection at schools which are over-subscribed in terms of being parents' first choice. Selectivity on the basis of religious, eductional or financial qualifications remains in the case of many voluntary-aided, direct grant and independent schools. Moreover, not all

[11]Change resulting from possible increased attendance at Further Education Colleges or Sixth Form Colleges is eliminated as the travel data relates only to children ages 11—15. Possible changes due to the raising of the school leaving age are thus also eliminated.

[12]Comprehensive schools accounted for under 40 per cent of maintained secondary schools in 1973 but for over 60 per cent in 1976.

[13]See J. P. Rigby and P. J. Hyde, *Journeys to school: a survey of secondary schools in Berkshire*, Transport and Road Research Laboratory, LR 776.

Table V.4   Walking to secondary schools in different areas, 1972/73 and 1975/76*

	NTS	Journeys on foot	Walk journeys in miles:		
			Less than ½ mile	½ but less than 1 mile	1 mile or more
		Per cent	*Per cent*		
All areas	72/73	55	38	35	26
	75/76	52	31	32	37
Metropolitan areas	72/73	59	41	29	30
	75/76	54	30	31	39
Other urban areas	72/73	57	35	39	26
	75/76	58	31	32	37
Rural areas	72/73	23	(18)	(7)	(2)
	75/76	20	29	40	31

*This table records the school journeys of pupils aged 11—15 years; figures in brackets are numbers where the sample is too small for analysis.

Local Education Authorities had restructured their secondary school system by 1976; neither, in other areas, had the comprehensive intake extended through all the school years. A further possible reason why walking did not increase is that restructuring has led to the introduction of split-site schools, with pupils attending the site nearest to their homes for only part of their school lives.

In addition, as with primary schools, there has been over time a persistent decline in the total number of schools and an increase in school roll size — above that which could be accounted for by population increase, the extension of sixth form education and the raising fo the school leaving age. Table V.5 indicates that rolls have increased by about 75 per cent since the mid-1960s. Between 1973 and 1976 the number of maintained secondary schools (including middle schools deemed as secondary) declined by three per cent, from 5,159 to 4,982. Again as with primary schools it is not known to what extent these changes are due to school closures — which in rural areas at least would lead to lengthier travel for most of the pupils concerned — or how much they are due to amalgamations of previously distinct administrative school units, which could but need not always lead to longer travel.

The effects of these changes have been felt by Education Authorities in the form of pressure exerted on budgets, with increasing numbers of pupils qualifying for free travel either in school buses or on normal stage carriage services. The problem has also been made more acute for some authorities because of the increasing costs of providing these public transport services to cater for what is a peaked market. For the pupils, too, and their parents, the

Table V.5   Changes in numbers of secondary schools and school roll size 1950—1975

| | Maintained secondary schools or departments*: | | | Middle schools deemed as secondary: | | |
	Number of schools or departments	Number of pupils	Pupils per school	Number of schools	Number of pupils	Pupils per school
	(000's)	(000's)		(000's)	(000's)	
1950	4.8	1,696	356	—	—	—
1955	5.1	1,915	372	—	—	—
1960	5.8	2,723	469	—	—	—
1965	5.9	2,819	481	—	—	—
1970	5.3	3,009	570	—	—	—
1975	4.6	3,619†	793†	0.1	37	348
				0.5	207	438

Source: DES, *Statistics of Education 1976, Vol. 1, Schools,* (England and Wales), HMSO 1977.
*Direct grant and independent schools (all ages) show similar trends.
†Increase partly a reflection of the raising of the school leaving age.

changes have meant increased costs where the distance to be travelled is over a practical walking distance but under the limit at which they qualify for free travel — normally three miles. Unfortunately, there is no data which show the extent of these costs, nor whether they deter pupils from low income households from staying at school above the mimimum leaving age. Neither is there any information available on any other social costs or effects which these changes might have had, such as influencing extra-curricular activity, friendship patterns and neighbourhood identity, or even indirectly influencing levels of alienation and vandalism.

VI Journey to Work

The journey to work is acknowledged as being the most heavily motorised journey purpose. It is also the one which has been taken as the starting point for the development of much transport policy and practice, owing to the problems it causes for transport planners, traffic managers and commuters themselves. Considerations relating to this journey are of paramount importance to those making decisions about urban road provision, and to those concerned with the development and management of public transport, not only in view of the needs of people without cars but also in areas of high car ownership where unbridled car use for the journey to work is undesirable. Discussion about catering for the journey to work is often couched, in fact, in terms of what is the right balance to be struck between the use of public and private travel methods — motorised methods, that is — in order to deal with the problem of too many vehicles making demands on the same road space at the same time.

This focus on the problems caused by heavy and concentrated motorised movement leads to the relevance of walking being overlooked; similarly the possibility of changing the total balance of travel (not just the motorised balance), and the consequence of doing so for resolving the problems currently posited by the journey to work, are not explored. Yet walking accounts for one in five journeys to work — a contribution almost equivalent to that made by public transport — and any change in this contribution affects the use of motorised methods and so is of significance for the demands made on the road network and on the public transport system.

This significance is not made apparent in official statistics for these do not generally incorporate data on walking or do so incompletely. For instance, Chapter I noted the way in which the 1971 Census places less emphasis on walking than other methods, and many transport planning documents use that part of the NTS which incorporates only walks of at least one mile. This practice has the effect of showing only one in fourteen work journeys as being made on foot, rather than the actual one in five. At the same time the car and public transport each appear to account for a greater share of the modal split, thereby biasing the *observed* balance of travel on this problematical journey. It is clearly risky for solutions to these problems to rely on controlling the change

66

in this observed balance, for there might be other, uncontrolled changes which occur as a result of shifts in the significance of walking. A reduction in walk journeys does not necessarily result in the proportional increase in car and public transport travel as would be needed if they were to retain their balance relative to each other. As far as can be seen from the NTS, relatively more journeys are added to car travel, thus offsetting any efforts that may be made to bring about a transfer from car to public transport.

Multi-purpose Journeys

In addition to the 15.5 thousand work journeys coded as such in the 1975/76 NTS, there were 1,541 journeys made from work to other destinations (not home), and coded according to the destination's purpose[1]; 44 per cent of these were on foot. Over 1,000 journeys to work (coded as such) were also multi-purpose (i.e. they originated somewhere other than home) and 35 per cent of these were on foot. Multi-purpose journeys thus account for 15 per cent of all travel to and from work. They are far more heavily walk orientated than are the simple journeys between home and work.

It is likely that much of the multi-purpose travel on foot takes place at lunch time — over two fifths is associated with journeys to and from shops and over one fifth with journeys to and from eating or drinking destinations — but it is not known whether this is by people who also walk to and from home. After shopping and eating or drinking, the next most common multi-purpose work journeys on foot are for personal business and those made in the course of work.[2] In the 1975/76 survey, there was an increase in multi-purpose journeys from somewhere else to work (on foot and by other methods) compared with the 1972/73 survey; it is not possible to say whether this represents an increase in multi-purpose journeys on the way to work from home or whether it represents more journeys back and forth from work in the course of the working day.

Pattern of Work Journeys

The distances walked from home to work are on average somewhat greater than for other journey purposes, but the walking speeds must be higher as the time taken is less than on other walk journeys.[3] On the whole, about one in fourteen of all work journeys involves walking less than half a mile from home, and one in nine involves less than fifteen minutes' walk.

The NTS findings underline the wider sphere of job opportunities opened up by the use of bus or car travel. The median distances travelled by these motorised methods is about four and a half miles, a distance which can give an area of opportunity of 14 square miles (in practice, the public transport traveller is restricted to the system's network). On the other hand, the median

---

[1] See Appendix A., para. 12.
[2] This is the most common multi-purpose journey by all methods, closely followed by shopping.
[3] Of work journeys on foot, 31 per cent are of one mile or more; 43 per cent take 15 mins. or more. For other journeys, 28 per cent of those on foot are of one mile or more, 53 per cent take 15 mins. or more.

walk is about three-quarters of a mile, a distance which encompasses an area of under 2½ square miles. These median figures imply that motor travel can provide a job market which is six times as extensive as that open to people who walk to work — though this will be conditioned by whether they live in areas primarily of residential land use or areas where job opportunities can be found on the doorstep or round the corner.

These wider opportunities are however partly gained at the expense of more time spent travelling, as Table VI.1 shows. Even so, the differences in travel time bear no relation to the differences in distance and related areal coverage. The median time of a car journey to work is just over 19 minutes, whereas for walking, the median is about 13 minutes; the car user's six-fold increase in job opportunities is thus achieved by only a one and a half-fold increase in travel time. People whose choice of travel to work lies between walking and public transport are not faced with such an attractive 'deal'; the public transport median time is about 33 minutes and, as noted above, the area of opportunity is restricted by the configuration of the network. Nevertheless, the time-cost of increasing job opportunities is lower for those travelling by public transport than for those on foot, for those using cars it is, of course, far lower.

Table VI.1 Distance and travel time on the journey to work, according to travel method

	Walk	Car	Public transport
	Per cent		
Distance:			
Under ½ mile	39	} 4	} 1
½ mile and under 1 mile	30		
1 mile and under 2 miles	27	15	14
2 or more miles	5	82	85
Time:			
Under 15 minutes	57	38	9
15 and under 30 minutes	33	42	33
30 or more minutes	9	20	58
Per cent of all work journeys by this method:*	19	45	17

* Exact travel method is unknown on a further 12 per cent of work journeys; what is clear is that this 12 per cent of journeys involves motorised travel.

Many transport planning exercises are concerned to reduce the time-cost of the journey to work, the saving often being brought about by traffic management measures or by road building or road improvement, the benefits of which accrue primarily to motorised travel. The effect of this is thus to save time for those—the motorised—who spend more of it, but not for those—the pedestrians—who get the least return. Moreover, if the concern is simply with the amount of time spent, rather than with its efficient use, then it would appear that benefits would arise from reducing mileage through land use measures, especially if they provide opportunities within an acceptable walking distance.

Table VI.2 Walking to work by men, women and teenagers, according to household car ownership

	2 or more	Cars in household One	None	All work journeys
		Per cent of work journeys on foot		
Teenagers (aged 16-20)	10	22	23	20
Women (aged 21-59)	10	27	41	28
Men (aged 21-64)	8	9	27	13
All working age people	9	16	31	19
		Per cent of walk journeys under 1 mile		
Teenagers (aged 16-20)	86	51	71	62
Women (aged 21-59)	82	70	70	72
Men (aged 21-64)	77	68	70	66
All working age people	79	67	62	68

In view of the trade-off between travel time and method, and job opportunity, it is interesting to compare the work journeys of men and women, bearing in mind also the difference in their level of access to motorised travel. Table VI.2 shows that men's journeys are more motor-oriented, even for many from non-car households, whose choice is with the poorer deal offered by public transport; clearly job opportunities are important to them. The same is also true of teenagers, though their lower level of access to the household car is reflected in more walking. Women in similar households have journeys which are more likely to be on foot and so shorter in time with restricted job opportunity, except in households with two cars where the woman's motorised option is probably the second car, rather than public transport as is the case for the great majority of women in households with no car or one car. Time is important to women; it can be seen that their walks are shorter as well, reflecting the additional responsibilities many of them have in the home. It is probable that these considerations effectively restrict the range and skill of jobs that they can take up—certainly their income levels are substantially below those of men, although the General Household Survey reports that women are more satisfied with their jobs.[4] The table also shows the effect of car ownership irrespective of age and sex, illustrating that almost one in three workers in households without a car walk to work, most of them being employed within a mile from their home.

---

[4] Office of Population Censuses and Surveys (OPCS), *The General Household Survey 1972*, HMSO, (1975).

Chapter III has shown that people in unskilled, low income households are likely to be without a car and, as well as income affecting their ability to afford a car, it could be that lack of a car inhibits them to some extent from seeking more skilled or higher paid work in a more extensive job market.[5] Some further indication of this complex relationship between jobs, skills, income and mobility can be seen from the PEP survey of the unemployed: this showed that walking to work was less common among people in employment than it had been among the unemployed in their previous job.[6] The survey showed that the higher the cost of the journey to work, the shorter had been the period of unemployment, but it was unable to quantify whether the ability to travel further—and so reach a wider job market—has the effect of reducing the period of unemployment. An earlier survey did, however, show that people who regain employment spend more time travelling to get to their new job.[7]

The relationship of walking to work with household income is shown in Table VI.3, together with the relationship for SEG ('blue' and 'white collar' households), in households without a car and with just one.[8] It indicates that the overall variation in travel by income and by SEG mainly—though not wholly—stems from differences in car ownership. Among men, neither income nor SEG affect the amount of walking if the household has a car, and they affect it relatively slightly if it does not have one; the difference, though slight, could result from non-car owners being more sensitive to the costs of travel by public transport than are car owners to the marginal cost of using their car. The overriding effect of the household car is less among women though it is still greater than the effect of household income and SEG. For teenagers however, none of these three household measures is apparently stronger than the others.

As a means of comparison with the figures given in Table VI.3 it is interesting to note the overall figures for journeys made on foot in each type of household. In low income households, 24 per cent of work journeys are made on foot, in 'blue collar' households, 23 per cent and in no car households, the figure is 32 per cent. In high income households, the comparable figure is 19 per cent, for 'white collar' households, it is 18 per cent and in one car households, 16 per cent.[9] Thus the variation by car ownership exceeds that by income or socio-economic group.

The lowest level of walking to work occurs in low density areas, though the influence of density is less for this journey purpose than for others. In high density areas 21 per cent of work journeys are made on foot; in low density areas the proportion is 15 per cent—a small variation compared with the difference in car ownership between the two types of area (59 per cent and 14

---

[5]A further factor is housing tenure: local authority tenants are less likely than owner occupiers to own cars. But not only is their day-to-day mobility thus more restricted, so is their residential mobility, making them yet more dependent on a smaller sphere of job opportunities.

[6]W. W. Daniel and E. Stilgoe, *Where are they now? A follow-up study of the unemployed.* PEP Broadsheet No. 546 (1974).

[7]W. W. Daniel, *A national survey of the unemployed,* PEP Broadsheet No. 546 (1974).

[8]Two car households are excluded from this analysis, for statistical reasons.

[9]The figures for low and high income, and for 'blue' and 'white collar' households exclude people in two car households.

Table VI.3 Walking to work according to household income, SEG* and car ownership

| | Work journeys made on foot: | | | |
	Men (aged 21-59)	Women (aged 21-64)	Teenagers (aged 16-20)	All
	Per cent			
No car in household:				
Head of household blue collar	28	45	23	32
Head of household white collar	24	40	29	31
One car in household:				
Head of household blue collar	9	30	23	17
Head of household white collar	9	24	23	15
No car in household:				
Head of household low income	29	42	29	33
Head of household high income	23	44	18	29
One car in household:				
Head of household low income	9	33	18	16
Head of household high income	9	25	24	16

*SEG of head of household. For definitions of SEG and income levels, see Appendix A, paras 12 and 19.

per cent of households without cars respectively). Better public transport clearly has an effect in the high density areas. Indeed, among people in households without a car the level of walking is highest in the areas of medium density, with public transport taking an increasing share of their travel, and lifts by car declining substantially, as density rises thereafter.

The NTS also allows the influence of the frequency of bus services to be measured; this shows that walking to work among non-car owners is less common in areas with frequent services.[10] The distances walked in these areas are also slightly shorter.

Changes in the Work Journey

There was less walking to work recorded in the 1975/76 NTS compared with the 1972/73 survey as Table VI.4 shows. The distances walked increased, however, which could imply a slight decline in the availability of local jobs.[11] Nevertheless, in spite of growing concern over the drop in local job opportunities in the inner areas of cities, walking in the metropolitan areas

---

[10] Better than half-hourly service: 28 per cent journeys are on foot, of which 70 per cent are walks of under 1 mile; half-hourly service or less often: 32 per cent work journeys on foot, of which 67 per cent are walks of under 1 mile.

[11] Changes in the workforce will also have influenced the pattern of travel but the entrance of more women into the workforce would, on past experience, have been expected to increase rather than to reduce the amount of walking.

Table VI.4   Walking to work, by area and distance, 1972/73 and 1975/76

	All areas	Metropolitan	Other urban	Rural
	Per cent of journeys on foot			
1972/73	21	20	22	22
1975/76	19	20	20	16
	*Per cent of journeys on foot which are less than 1 mile**			
1972/73	72	70	72	85
1975/76	69	69	66	81

*The percentage figure of all walk journeys under ½ mile in 1972/73 was 43; in 1975/76 it was 39.

hardly changed. The amount of walking declined most in rural areas, and the distances walked increased most in non-metropolitan urban areas, possibly reflecting changes in public transport fares and levels of service.

The changes shown in the NTS indicate a continuation of the trends seen in the Census which showed that between 1966 and 1971 the proportion of workers who walked to work fell from 24 per cent to 20 per cent. This was matched particularly by an increase in car travel. Distances travelled lengthened, with the number of people commuting from one local authority to another increasing by four per cent.

The decline shown by comparison of the 1972/73 and 1975/76 surveys conceals the fact that in another part of the 1975/76 survey four per cent of all the employed population reported that because of increases in public transport fares they now walk more, the journeys affected being their journeys to work. This proportion would be much higher (an approximate estimate would be 15 per cent) if it could be based on the number of workers who used public transport in the first place.

The fares increases affected teenagers most (irrespective of household car ownership): over 7 per cent reported a transfer to walking as did between 5 and 6 per cent of working men and women in households without a car, and of non-driving women in households with a car. Men and women with a licence and their own car were hardly affected; some changed their travel to work because of petrol price rises and this resulted in a slight increase in walking, but it had less effect on them than the fares increases had on other workers.

It is not clear how much of this particular increase in walking represents a transfer of a complete journey (either to the same or to a different workplace), and how much it represents a transfer of just part of a journey (getting off the bus one stop earlier to avoid a fare stage). The extent to which it is a complete transfer is of relevance in analysing changes in modal split on this journey.

Cuts in public transport, as opposed to increases in fares, appear to have had much less effect on walking to work, just one per cent of non-car owners reported an increase in walking for this reason. But it is not possible to determine how much of the increase in car ownership, and so in car use for the journey to work, has been influenced by the decline or withdrawal of public transport services.

The findings in this chapter underline the need to include walking in exercises such as those calculating, or attempting to control, modal split. Thus, while a comparison of NTS data for 1972/73 and 1975/76 shows that public transport use declined and that car use increased by roughly the same amount, it should not be concluded that this represented a transfer from one to the other. The findings on the change in walking, and on the impact of fares increases, would suggest a more complex change in the modal balance, involving for some people a transfer from public transport to walking and for other people (and for other reasons) a transfer from walking as well as from public transport to car travel.

VII Shopping

It has been seen that, in terms of frequency, shopping is the second most common journey, accounting for one in five of the journeys that people make.[1] In the context of walking the significance of these journeys is apparent from the fact that nearly half of them are made on foot[2] and that they represent one quarter of all journeys on foot. Both the frequency with which shopping journeys are made and the proportion of them made on foot hardly varies by time of year: there are only slight increases in the autumn and slight decreases in the winter.

Table VII.1   Distribution of shopping journeys by distance and travel method

Distance	Per cent of all shopping journeys:		Per cent of all shopping journeys in this distance band made on foot
	on foot	all methods	
Less than 1 mile	38	42	90
1 mile but less than 2	10	22	45
2 miles but less than 3	2	11	15
3 miles but less than 5	(—)†	11	2
5 or more miles	(—)†	14	(—)†
All distances*	46	100	46

*Including journeys for which no distance was recorded.
† Indicates that the percentage is less than 0.5.

As Table VII.1 shows, the great majority (90 per cent) of shorter shopping journeys are made on foot. Indeed, this is the method of travel of three quarters of the journeys covering less than two miles—which represent two-thirds of all shopping journeys.

---

[1] In the NTS, journeys are classified as shopping irrespective of whether anything was bought; journeys made by children accompanying adults to shops were also included. However, journeys to 'service' shops, such as hairdressers, were recorded separately as personal business.

[2] This significance is almost wholly unappreciated in the published NTS tables for, by excluding journeys on foot of under one mile, over one third of all shopping journeys and about three-quarters of all the ones made on foot are lost.

The local nature of much shopping activity is all the more apparent from a closer look at short journeys, for this shows that one quarter of all shopping journeys are both on foot and less than half a mile long. In common with most types of journey, over half are made in less than 15 minutes, the median being 13 minutes.

The strong association between people's level of access to a car (the simplest measure of which in the NTS is whether respondents live in a household with or without a car, and whether they can drive) and their pattern of travel has been seen repeatedly in this study. It is no less true of shopping; people in households without a car make two-thirds of these journeys on foot, for those with a car the proportion is halved. Similarly, licence holders in car owning households make half the proportion of these journeys on foot compared with the proportion for all other adults.

Age and Sex

A closer examination of the shopping patterns of different age and sex groups shows little variation among children and teenagers, both making only two or three journeys a week on average. Half of these journeys are made on foot, perhaps reflecting the fact that much of what they can afford—sweets, toys, comics and so on—can usually be purchased in small shops near their home, and that they often run errands there for their mothers. The influence of car ownership on their journeys is not as marked as it is on their parents, clearly because they can only go by car as passengers. Nevertheless, it is still strong: in households with two or more cars children and teenagers make about one third of their shopping journeys on foot, in households with one car the proportion reduces to nearly a half, whilst in households with no car, nearly two-thirds of teenagers' trips and three-quarters of children's are made on foot.

Men of working age are also comparatively infrequent shoppers, likewise making two or three journeys for this purpose each week. But nearly three-quarters of them have a driving licence and thus only one in five of their shopping journeys are made on foot. Men pensioners are more frequent shoppers than younger men but less likely to have a car, so they make about half of their four journeys a week on foot.

Women Shoppers

Women are the most relevant group to examine in the context of shopping in view of their traditional role as the household's principal shopper. It is not surprising to find that they make twice as many journeys for this purpose as other people, that is, an average of five a week. However, in spite of the fact that nearly three-quarters of women of working age live in car-owning households, half of their shopping journeys are made on foot.

Table VII.2 shows that the frequency with which women shop varies little according to the level of their access to a car, though it has a marked influence on the extent of their walking on these journeys. Those with neither a licence nor a household car rely on walking for two thirds of their journeys whereas

Table VII.2 Daily journey rates and modal split for women's shopping journeys, by age and access to a car

	Journeys per person per day:		Per cent of journeys on foot	Per cent of walk journeys of less than ½ mile
	on foot	all methods		
Age 21-59 years:				
No licence, no car	0.44	0.69	64	49
No licence, 1 or more cars	0.38	0.76	50	48
Licence, 1 car	0.26	0.71	37	43
Licence, 2 or more cars	0.14	0.72	20	46
Age 60 or over:				
No car	0.36	0.69	61	50
1 or more cars	0.25	0.65	39	41
All groups	0.33	0.68	49	47

those with their own car and a licence rely on walking for only one in five of them. It might be thought that those who walk more would walk further, to get to a wider range of shopping opportunities but this is not so—there is clearly a disincentive to walk a long way when carrying shopping. This means, in turn, that they rely on shops within one mile of home for over half of their shopping needs and for shops within half a mile for one third or more of their shopping needs.

The table shows too that women pensioners in non-car owning households make slightly fewer trips on foot than do younger women. It could be that this is due to the availability of concessionary fares to many pensioners, which would encourage them to travel more by bus.

Women who go out to work make only about two-thirds as many shopping journeys as housewives, and considerably fewer of their journeys are on foot, as Table VII.3 shows.[3] It might be thought that this was a result of the different mobility levels of the two groups of women—the NTS shows that housewives are less likely to be able to drive. However, the table shows that their shopping patterns differ within each mobility group, indicating that shopping journeys and local shops play a somewhat different role in the lives of women who go out to work.

The difference between housewives and those going out to work may reflect the restrictive effect of children. Walking is easier than bus travel for women who often have to cope with a pram or push-chair as well as the shopping, if they are accompanied by young children. As far as housewives in households with one car are concerned, the difference may also be accounted for by the

---

[3]To avoid the influence on these shopping patterns of pensioners' different life styles, only the journeys of women aged 21-59 have been included.

Table VII.3   Proportion of shopping journeys on foot, according to whether gainfully employed and access to a car

	No driving licence			Licence holder			All women (21-59 years)
	Number of cars in household:			Number of cars in household:			
	None	One	2 or more	None	One	2 or more	
	Per cent journeys on foot			*Per cent journeys on foot*			*Per cent journeys on foot*
Housewife	69	58	50	74	48	16	54
Employed*	59	43	42	42	28	24	40

*Outside the home, either part or full time.

car not being available during the day when it is convenient for them to go shopping. In non-car owning households it is worth noting, too, that women who are not working are likely to live on lower incomes so that the cost of fares, particularly if children have to be paid for, may act as a deterrent to bus travel and thereby encourage more walking.

Bus Services

It might be expected that in areas where there are better bus services, non-car owners' shopping journeys on foot would be appreciably shorter as shoppers would be more encouraged to go by bus to reach the larger but more distant shopping centres with their typically wider range and lower cost of goods. This is hardly confirmed in an analysis of the NTS, for the walking journeys of non-car owners are only marginally shorter where bus services are more frequent. It might be expected, too, that more frequent services would result in a lower proportion of non-car owners' shopping journeys being made on foot; in fact there is a marginal increase in areas with the more frequent services. Similarly, it could be presumed that the availability of concessionary fares to some pensioners would encourage them to use the bus when shopping, thereby reducing the extent of their journeys on foot for this purpose, but though those with such concessions do make twice as many shopping journeys by motorised travel, they also make twice as many journeys on foot, as pensioners without concessions.

In each of these instances, it is apparent that variations in the character of public transport do not have the expected effect on the distance travelled when shopping on foot, or on the frequency of these journeys. The reason is that there are other factors which affect walking, one of which is accessibility. This can be examined through its relationship with settlement size and population density, and through their relationship with the pattern of walking, bearing in mind the fact that bus services improve and concessionary fares are more widely available in large cities and so in areas of higher density.

Density and Settlement Size

There is almost no difference in the proportion of shopping journeys made on foot in metropolitan and other urban areas but in rural areas the proportion is lower. Further analysis confirms the strong link noted earlier of household car ownership with population density and with the pattern of walking. As Table VII.4 shows, the proportion of these journeys on foot—that is one third—in the lowest density band is half of that in the highest, and the fairly steady increase with density matches the decrease in household car ownership.

Table VII.4   Pattern of shopping journeys on foot, according to population density

	Population density*										All density bands
	1	2	3	4	5	6	7	8	9	10	
Per cent of journeys on foot	32	38	44	43	44	45	48	50	54	66	46
Per cent of people in car households	79	76	66	69	65	66	59	56	50	40	63
Per cent with grocer within 6 minutes walk	52	59	67	68	67	74	74	77	79	84	70
Non-car households per cent journeys on foot	58	56	59	66	61	61	66	63	60	68	62

*1 = lowest density; 10 = highest density.

The data in the table also suggest strongly that the accessibility of shopping facilities plays a part in altering the method of travel which people use to get to them. When the journeys of people solely from non-car owning households are examined it can be seen that as density increases, so does the proportion of households with a grocer nearby and so does the increase in the proportion of journeys made on foot.

The influence of proximity is, however, partly countered where a wider choice of opportunities is available somewhat further away and accessible by the better bus services found in such areas—or, indeed, where such opportunities are still within practicable walking distance. Thus Table VII.5 shows that journeys on foot are, on average, longer in higher density areas where such opportunities exist within a mile or two. The attraction of better facilities appears to encourage shoppers to walk further than their nearest shops; the additional effort, which enables them to reach the better facilities on foot in higher density areas, is compensated for by being able to reach the larger and more varied shops.

Changes in the Pattern of Walk Journeys

Whereas in both the NTS of 1972/73 and of 1975/76 shopping represents 20 per cent of all journeys, comparison of data in the two surveys reveals a

Table VII.5   Access to chain store, and long walk journeys for shopping, according to population density

	Population density band										All density bands
	1	2	3	4	5	6	7	8	9	10	
Per cent with chain store in 14-43 min walk	12	14	27	35	44	45	57	55	56	49	42
Per cent of walk journeys of 1 mile or more	19	17	19	22	30	27	23	27	25	26	24

decline of about 9 per cent in the proportions of these journeys made on foot. This is the largest decline of all the journey purposes. The decline is most marked in rural areas where the 16 per cent drop no doubt reflects the dramatic increase of 12 per cent in household car ownership in these areas between the surveys. However, changes in access to cars by no means wholly explains the decline here or in the metropolitan areas, where there was only a one per cent increase in household car ownership in the three years, yet a fifteen per cent drop in the proportion of journeys made on foot. This suggests that shoppers are choosing or having to travel further to the shops they use.

It might be expected that this would result both in longer journeys on foot as well as in less walking, and indeed, the comparison of figures on these two aspects in Table VII.6 confirms that this is so. Even if the shortest journeys of under a quarter of a mile are excluded on the grounds that the decline seen in the 1975/76 data may partly be explained by the exclusion in that survey of journeys of less than 50 yards, then it can still be calculated, for the next shortest distance band, that the decline between the two surveys in the proportion of walk journeys, was nearly ten per cent.

Some of these changes between the surveys are attributable to increases in household car ownership and in people learning to drive; some would also

Table VII.6   Comparison of distances travelled on foot for shopping in 1972/73 and 1975/76

Distance	Per cent of journeys on foot	
	1972/73	1975/76
Less than ¼ mile	34	27
¼ mile but less than ½ mile	25	21
½ mile but less than ¾ mile	21	22
¾ mile but less than 1 mile	5	5
1 mile or more	15	24
All distances	55	46

have resulted from the fact that the 1975/76 survey included more people living in low density areas. However, when these variations are taken into account, as in Table VII.7, walking is still seen to have declined. The sharpest drop according to density is in the lowest band, particularly for people without a car.

Table VII.7 Proportion of shopping journeys made on foot by women, according to household car ownership

| | Population density band | | | | |
	Low	Low-medium	Medium-high	High	All density bands
	Per cent journeys on foot				
Women in households with:					
No car 1972/73	72	78	74	77	75
1975/76	54	80	72	72	71
One car 1972/73	52	56	64	75	59
1975/76	51	50	60	67	56

Data from the two surveys do not allow examination of any possible relationship between the amount of walking on shopping journeys and changes in the accessibility of shops, as no record was made of accessibility in the 1972/73 survey. However, other sources, notably the *Census of Distribution and Other Services,* provide evidence which indicates a slow eroding process of closure year by year of many small shops owing to decline in the profitability of family businesses, to comprehensive redevelopment or to the rationalising and economising programme of the major national retail chains. As a result there are today far fewer of the type of shop likely to be easily accessible on foot.[4] The changes which have taken place in retailing have led to large reductions in the number of small shops, and increases in the number of large shops which are accessible by motorised travel, rather than by walking.

Table VII.8 shows the most recent data on the number of shops recorded in the 1971 Census and compares these with equivalent figures from the 1961 Census. It can be seen that in the period of only ten years, the number of shops declined by 17 per cent, and this at a time when the number of persons employed per shop rose fairly sustantially in every sector of the trade, reflecting the increase in the size of shops.[5] Other evidence suggests that there

[4] For instance, International Stores has recently reported that it has pruned the number of its stores from 1,100 to 717; yet even in the one year when the number dropped by 8 per cent, the floor space went up by 25 per cent. See Christopher Wilkins, 'Price cuts may force some stores to close' *The Times,* 1st February 1978.
[5] DoE Circular 96/97 on 'Large New Stores' records the fact that whilst the number of hypermarkets and superstores is only 1.7 per cent of all retail outlets, they cover 10 per cent of the total floor area.

are many external factors impinging on the viability of the smaller retail chains and independent local shops which will tend to accelerate this process of recent years. For instance, there has been a price-cutting war between the major retail chains together with the widespread introduction of a sliding scale of charges by wholesalers which effectively discriminates against shopkeepers with low turnovers. The consequence of the decline in the fortunes of the smaller shops is that their share of sales of groceries and provisions has fallen from 52 per cent in 1961 to an estimated 38 per cent in 1974.

Table VII.8   Changes in the numbers of shops and employees, 1961-1971

Retail trade sector:	Number of shops		Per cent change	Employees per shop	
	1961	1971	1961-71	1961	1971
	000's			Number	
Cooperatives	29	15	-48	6.7	8.6
Multiples	67	67	0	9.5	12.2
Independents	446	391	-12	3.7	4.1
Grocery and provisions	147	105	-28	3.8	5.1
Other food retailing	115	93	-19	4.1	4.5
Confect./newsagent/etc.	70	52	-26	3.6	5.3
All these sectors	874	723	-17	4.3	5.2

Source: Annual Abstract of Statistics, HMSO, (1977), Table 11.1.

Multi-purpose Journeys

About one in six shopping trips is made on the way to or from some other activity—most commonly work or social visits. Nearly half the multi-purpose shopping journeys are made on foot, those most typically associated with walking being travel between shops and school, and between shops and work; almost two thirds of these types of journey are on foot. At the other extreme, only one third of the travel between shops and social visits is on foot.

Multi-purpose shopping journeys declined slightly between the two NTS surveys, those made on foot declining more than those made by other travel methods. This was mainly due to a drop in the combination of shopping with 'other shopping', perhaps reflecting a decline in the opportunities for making this type of multi-purpose journey on foot, owing to shop closures. On the other hand, it may partly reflect a broadening of the range of goods sold under one roof. [6]

Notwithstanding these multi-purpose journeys, it would appear that walking is relied on for much shopping—even among the minority of shoppers

[6] Some of this decline is likely to be attributable to the exclusion of journeys on foot of less than 50 yards from the 1975/76 NTS, although it should be noted that respondents were instructed to treat a shopping journey encompassing adjacent shops as only one journey.

who can drive a car. However, comparison of the travel records in the two surveys shows walking to have declined more sharply for shopping than for any other journey purpose but the average length of journeys on foot to have increased. The reduction in the proportion of short walking journeys for shopping is most marked in the low density areas where the combined effect of rising car ownership and licence holding—and possibly of reductions in the number of retail outlets—is greatest. These facts combined with evidence on the decline in the number of shops suggests that people with and without cars are choosing to, or having to make more of shopping journeys by motorised means and, where they still go on foot, making them over somewhat longer distances.

VIII   Personal Business

Personal business covers a wide variety of activities, from hospital appointments to visits to betting shops. Some journeys are connected with financial transactions of one kind or another, for example at post offices, banks or social security offices; others are associated with the range of activities covered by the statutory and voluntary social services—the latter involving the travel of both workers and recipients of these services. Locations for personal business may be scattered or grouped in town centres; they may be locally based or involve cross-town travel. For some personal business there is a choice of destinations, some is associated with one particular venue. For some aspects, economic or administrative considerations have led to changes in the pattern of provision and the rationalising of facilities or services provided, possibly with consequences for their location and access and thereby for the travel of their users.

Personal business travel usually involves fairly essential activity—collecting pensions, visiting doctors or clinics, attending meetings, paying bills and attending funerals or other church services. However, not everyone needs to attend to all the different types of personal business; and there is also a certain element of choice in whether people are involved in some activities, in the frequency of travel involved, or in the location used.

Personal Business Travel

These journeys account for ten per cent of all travel, equivalent to 24 journeys per day for every 100 people. Men pensioners are the most active in this respect, and children the least. There is a little more walking on these journeys than on the average journey, 38 per cent being on foot (9 journeys per day for every 100 people), and the walks are of slightly less than average length, 75 per cent being under one mile.[1] For adults, walking is more common than on the journey to work, though less common than on shopping journeys.

A comparison of the 1972/73 and 1975/76 NTS shows the by now familiar pattern of relatively less walking and longer walks in the 1975/76 survey as can be seen in Table VIII.1.

---

[1] The ratio of car to public transport (excluding journeys for which the method is unknown) is 4.4:1—that is slightly more car oriented than average.

Table VIII.1 Pattern of personal business journeys on foot, 1972/73 and 1975/76

	Length of journeys on foot:				Walk as per cent of all methods	Number of journeys per person per day:	
	Less than ¼ mile	¼ mile but less than ½ mile	½ mile but less than 1 mile	1 mile and over		walk	all methods
	Per cent						
1972/73	30	24	29	17	41	0.09	0.22
1975/76	25	20	30	26	38	0.09	0.24

The median walk distance is about half a mile, whereas the median journey for cars is about three miles, and for public transport just over three miles. Just over half the walk journeys take under 15 minutes—similar to car travel although, of course, covering much less distance. The substantially longer travel times required for using public transport means that the median travel time is almost doubled for people who cannot or choose not to reach their destination on foot and who do not have the option of using a car. Only four per cent of the journeys on foot for personal business are over two miles, and twelve per cent take thirty minutes or longer.

It could be said that the true extent of travel associated with personal business is higher than that shown at first glance in the NTS for two reasons.

Escorting

First, the five per cent of all journeys whose purpose is recorded as 'escorting' could be viewed as being within the category of personal business; mothers taking their children to school or to the doctor, and adults or neighbours giving elderly parents a lift somewhere, are typical examples. Escorting is by no means always by car: 29 per cent of such journeys are on foot, generally to local destinations such as school and occasionally parks or other places for outdoor recreation. The distances walked are short—almost half are under half a mile. Escorting was reported slightly more often in the 1975/76 NTS than in the earlier one, though the proportion of journeys on foot remained the same.

Multi-purpose journeys

The second reason for suggesting that the recorded amount of personal business travel is underestimated is that, on multi-purpose journeys[2] only one journey purpose is recorded—that undertaken at the journey's destination, not its origin. Therefore, personal business activity is excluded from the record if it is followed by travel to some other activity—from bank to shops, or from hospital visit to a friend's or relative's home. If these journeys were to be coded as personal business (rather than as the end of journey purpose) then its

[2]Journeys which neither begin nor end at home—see Appendix A para 12.

share of all travel would rise from 9 to 10 per cent, although the proportion of journeys on foot would remain the same.

Analysis of the association of multi-purpose travel with each journey purpose shows that personal business activity is quite prominent (irrespective of whether the personal business is the first or second activity concerned): one in six personal business activities are on the way to or from somewhere else. Of the connecting journeys, 36 per cent are made on foot, most commonly to or from shops and particularly to shops indicating, for example, a visit to a bank or to collect a pension followed by some shopping. The next most likely combination is personal business undertaken on the way to or from work. It is very probable, though it is not known precisely to what extent, that some people who travel to work by car or public transport (as well as those who walk to work) make use of facilities located near to their place of work at lunch time or after work. Other combinations of activities with personal business are less significant; social visits head the list but the travel involved is half the level for travel between personal business and shopping or work, as the location of personal business activity is less likely to be conveniently near someone else's home. It is relevant to note here that for car travel, personal business is associated with social visits more than with any other activity.

In the 1972/73 NTS one in five journeys for personal business were made in association with another activity, with 45 per cent of these being on foot. Though the numbers are too small for detailed analysis it would appear that the decline in walking by 1975/76 was strongest for multi-purpose travel between personal business and shopping and for journeys linking two types of personal business — for instance, a visit to the doctor followed by a call into the post office, or an appointment at the town hall followed by a payment of a gas bill. There was also a decline in walking where personal business was combined with leisure or social activities, though there was an increase in walking between personal business and work.

Variation in People's Travel

On personal business journeys as recorded (i.e. excluding the two categories already mentioned) variation in the patterns of travel of people with and without cars is similar to that for other journey purposes. More walking and longer walks are reported by people in households without a car, though their catchment area by all travel methods is more restricted and the number of journeys they make by all methods is lower.

Walking is more common among pensioners than other adults not only in terms of the proportion of journeys on foot but also their number. For men pensioners the journey rates on foot and by all travel methods are substantially higher than for other age groups as Table VIII.2 shows. One feature of this activity for pensioners is pension collection, and an earlier PEP survey[3] has shown that two out of three pensioners visit a post office to collect their pension every week, that men go there rather more often than their wives and

---

[3]M. Hillman et al, *Transport Realities and Planning Policy,* op.cit.

Table VIII.2 Daily journey rates and modal split for personal business journeys, by age, sex and household car ownership

| | Journeys per person per day: | | Journeys |
	on foot	all methods	on foot
			Per cent
Children (3-10 years)	0.07	0.19	39
Teenagers (11-19 years)	0.12	0.26	45
Men (16-64)	0.06	0.24	25
Women (16-60)	0.09	0.24	36
Men (65 and over)	0.15	0.32	47
Women pensioners (60 and over)	0.12	0.23	52
Cars in household:			
None	0.12	0.21	55
One	0.08	0.26	32
Two or more	0.05	0.25	22

that over three quarters walk. Visits to health facilities are another important aspect of personal business for pensioners.

The high level of walking among pensioners relates to those with a concessionary pass for bus travel as well as to those without one. In fact, the former make more journeys on foot than do the latter, though they make slightly more motorised ones as well.

A mixed picture emerges when personal business travel is viewed in relation to income and socio-economic group. Men and women of working age in low income households walk more than those in high income households, as might be expected in view of the differences in car ownership. Indeed, when controlled by car ownership,[4] the effect of income on travel is much reduced, though the number of personal business journeys (by all methods) is higher for those with low incomes, possibly due in part to their lower telephone ownership or to such things as variations in methods of making and receiving payments (cash over the counter rather than cheques by post or bankers order). However, these factors do not appear to affect the travel of people in different SEGs in the way that might be expected. Instead, the NTS shows that people from 'white collar' households make a greater number of personal business journeys. More surprisingly still, they make more journeys and more of their journeys on foot, in spite of higher levels of car ownership.[5] The data offer no explanation for this: it could be that the SEG affects the type of personal business conducted and the locations which have to be visited. It is also possible that adults in 'white collar' occupations have opportunities for personal business nearer their places of work which are more convenient for visiting on foot at lunch time or after work.

[4, 5]This analysis was carried out for people in households with no car or with just one car, those with two or more cars were excluded for statistical reasons.

Area Differences

The lowest level of walking (29 per cent on foot) for personal business journeys occurs in the areas of lowest density, among both car owners and non-car owners. The highest level of walking (50 per cent on foot) is in the top two density categories, and the effect of density is particularly visible for people in car owning households (who nevertheless walk less than people in lower densities who have no car). In both extremes of density the walk journeys are shorter than the average, and in the middle densities (where on average 37 per cent of these journeys are made on foot), there is little consistency in the distance walked.

Analysis by settlement size shows a similar variation: in rural areas there is less walking and shorter than average walks, and the journey rate by all travel methods is relatively high, as Table VIII.3 shows. A comparison between the two surveys shows that the common characteristic for all areas is a lengthening of walk journeys in the later survey. Other measures of change are not consistent for all areas—in the rural areas longer walks are accompanied by a

Table VIII.3 **Pattern of personal business journeys on foot, 1972/73 and 1975/76, by type of area**

	Metropolitan areas	Other urban areas	Rural areas	All areas
	Per cent			
Journeys on foot:				
1972/73	43	42	25	41
1975/76	40	39	30	38
Journeys of 1 mile or more				
1972/73	22	15	3	17
1975/76	29	25	22	26
	Number			
Journeys per person per day:				
on foot				
1972/73	0.094	0.094	0.066	0.092
1975/76	0.084	0.098	0.068	0.090
1 or more miles on foot:				
1972/73	0.021	0.014	0.002	0.025
1975/76	0.024	0.025	0.015	0.013
motorised*				
1972/73	0.122	0.128	0.193	0.132
1975/76	0.129	0.152	0.162	0.148

*Motorised includes a small amount of cycling.

drop in motorised travel and in the total number of journeys per person, so that by 1975/76, the proportion of journeys on foot had increased. In urban areas, on the other hand, the longer walks are accompanied by more motor travel and a decrease in the proportion of journeys on foot and also, in the metropolitan areas, in their number.

The NTS includes information on the accessibility of certain facilities associated with personal business travel, and the survey also shows that there is a strong linkage between accessibility and population density. The linkage between density and travel to personal business is much less strong, implying that a certain amount of choice exists and is exercised as to the use of facilities.[6] It is not possible to isolate the separate strands of personal business travel and it is not possible, therefore, to asses how much the different types of facility are tied to different people, areas and pattern of travel; nor is it possible to tell how influential accessibility is on those patterns. However, it is possible, or rather logical, to state that changes in travel will result from changes in the locations of facilities or in their pattern of provision—factors which also affect their accessibility.

Unfortunately, it is not possible to test this supposition because information about access was not included in the 1972/73 NTS; if it is included in future surveys it will then be possible to compare changes in access with changes in travel. In some instances, it will also be possible to view changes in provision, using official records, against changes in access and travel as reported by respondents. Such comparisons are clearly necessary to ensure that decisions taken for economic or management reasons do not have unintended effects on travel and so on the public's use of facilities provided for them. These matters are of concern both to those involved with land use and transport planning and to those more particularly involved in the provision and administration of the relevant facilities. Clearly again, a full flow of information between these two groups is also needed to enable comparisons to be made.

Information on provision is not readily available for all the facilities which generate personal business travel, though it does exist for some of the facilities whose access is recorded in the NTS. The rest of this chapter looks at two examples and discusses the reasons for, and implications of, changes in the networks of publicly used facilities. The first example is the post office network, the second is health services—both examples being associated with wide-ranging and necessary personal business travel among the whole population.[7]

Changes in the Post Office Network

A great deal of personal business is carried out at post offices: it is of a varied nature with only about one third of it constituting actual postal business. The rest is concerned with the payment of various pensions, orders

---

[6]See Chapter IV.

[7]The authors would like to acknowledge the help and information given by the Post Office (Operations Department) and the Pharmaceutical Society of Great Britain, and to stress that any opinions expressed here are the authors' and are not necessarily concurred in by either of those two bodies.

and benefits, the issue of licences, savings, payments through GIRO (for example, local authority rents), and other matters in which the post office acts as an agent for the department or body concerned. For example, there are about 8 million people in receipt of retirement pensions, the great majority of which are paid through the post office and collected on a weekly basis.[8] In total an average of over 11 million pensions (retirement and other) were paid out each week in 1975 and there are almost 4.5 million families in receipt of child benefit.

About 23,000 post offices deal with this business, of which about 21,000 are the smaller, sub-post offices traditionally found in 'corner-shop' sites within residential areas, in local shopping parades and in villages. These offices, and some of the Crown offices (which are not all in town centres), provide a facility which is recognised as filling a local need in many areas, acting as a social focus and providing a point of contact for the surrounding community—as well as commonly being located close to shops or indeed, being combined with shopping facilities.

The NTS shows that 80 per cent of households have a post office within 13 minutes' walk, this proportion ranging from 88 per cent in London to 64 per cent in rural areas. Variations in access within cities also occur according to the density of the neighbourhood: thus 91 per cent of households living at the highest density are within 13 minutes' walk of a post office compared to about 70 per cent in low densities (excluding the very low density rural areas). Earlier PEP surveys[9] (in the Outer Metropolitan Areas of South East England) showed that 77 per cent of pensioners walk when collecting pensions and 73 per cent of younger women walk to post offices. Where the younger women had a post office within ten minutes' walk, this proportion rose to 78 per cent.

Post offices are thus among the most local of facilities. (Of the six facilities examined in the NTS, grocers' shops were the most local, with post offices second on the list). It is interesting that this information which is 'consumer-based' originated from the Department of Transport, rather than from the Post Office itself: the Post Office has information on the number of offices, their financial status and the business transacted but not on their access to consumers, though it should be added that changes are only made after considering the accessibility and travel of users, especially pensioners.

When changes in provision do occur they are more likely to be closures of existing offices than the opening of new ones, so reducing the overall level of access. The number of offices fell by almost one thousand between 1973 and 1977, at an average rate of about one per cent of the total each year, or a loss of nearly five offices a week, the rate being higher in the later years than earlier.[10] Although Crown offices only fell from 1,620 to 1,581, sub-post offices were most affected, their numbers falling from 22,472[11] in 1973, to 21,543 in 1977. Actual closures were higher still, but were offset by the

---

[8] About half a million pensions are paid through banks.
[9] M. Hillman et al, *Transport Realities and Planning Policy*, op.cit.
[10] Source: correspondence with the Operations Department, Postal Headquarters.
[11] Excludes 38 offices subsequently transferred to the Isle of Man administration.

establishment of some new offices, usually in areas of residential expansion or urban renewal. In 1977, for instance, about 30 offices were opened, and well over 200 closed.

The Post Office does not take the implications of this trend lightly, for it aims to give careful consideration to the needs of users, and is aware of the importance of local access to young mothers, to the increasing population of elderly people, and of the fact that the population is spread over an ever widening area with the consequences that this has for accessibility. It is also aware of other bodies' concern about the effect of closures on extending travel distances: 'the storm of protest which often greets a proposal to close a post office most commonly arises from the fear that additional problems will be caused to the old and the immobile . . .' (the Post Office includes mothers who have to travel with young children in this category).[1][2]

These concerns were expressed by several bodies in their evidence to the Post Office Review Committee (the Carter Committee). The Association of District Councils (ADC) and the Association of Metropolitan Authorities (AMA) both stressed the need to consider problems of access for pedestrians, including distance and road crossing, when planning or rationalising the provision of post office counter services. These Associations as well as Age Concern made particular reference to the problems of elderly and infirm people, who are among the regular users of post offices. The Post Office Users' National Committee (POUNC) also noted that 'it is the less mobile or disabled members of the public who are most likely to be seriously inconvenienced by the loss of a post office'. The National Federation of Women's Institutes expressed the further view that problems caused by post office closures can be exacerbated by the decline in public transport in urban as well as rural areas. Where bus services exist they may be infrequent and expensive to use; moreover, it should be noted that concessionary fares for pensioners are not always available in rural areas; closure of a post office in these areas may necessitate relatively lengthy and expensive bus travel.

There are two main reasons for closures, most of which occur when a sub-postmastership falls vacant; either it stems from a deliberate decision by the Post Office, or from difficulty in recruiting someone to fill the vacancy. In both situations there is a review which takes account of the accepted locational guidelines for provision but also considers the needs of the local community and the nature of journeys to alternative offices (the hilliness of the area and the difficulty of road crossing are two examples), as well as considering the relative costs of retaining or closing the post office. The guidelines relate, on the face of it, to access—closure being considered if the office is less than one mile from another one in an urban area or less than two miles from its nearest 'neighbour' in the more populous of the rural areas. These guidelines also apply when a decision is taken on whether to open a new office in an area of expanding population or housing. However, applying similar guidelines for opening and closing offices can have very different results for the population

---

[12] Cmnd 6850, Report of the Post Office Review Committee, Chairman C. F. Carter, HMSO, (1977).

affected, because the guidelines suggest a minimum distance between offices, rather than a maximum distance travelled by users. Rigid adherence to the guidelines could thus imply, on closure, extending travel to over one mile in urban areas and to over two miles in rural areas.

In practice, the Post Office tempers these guidelines by reference to local factors, and closure as a matter of policy is usually restricted to urban areas. In rural areas 'local factors' are more compelling, but there are sometimes difficulties in finding people to take the job of sub-postmaster—especially as the financial rewards are often small. Nearby towns tend to act as 'magnets' for the commercial and shopping activity of those people who are more mobile, leaving the village facility—often a post office with shop attached—with a declining but dependent regular clientèle, plus a number of irregular users. Indeed, the post office counters opposition to closure in such instances with publicity along the lines of ' . . . if you want to keep it use it!'

The relatively small amount of business conducted at some of the rural offices threatened with closure when a vacancy arises would seem to suggest that a flexible attitude towards part time opening is needed—a less remunerative business would be more attractive if the amount of work involved was also less. Alternatively it is sometimes suggested that mobile offices could be used to serve different places on different days—perhaps with fixed offices but mobile sub-postmasters. The Carter Committee considered that this suggestion would imply replacing several fixed, full time offices in one area at the same time—a development which would be undesirable. However there is clearly scope for less drastic arrangements, such as a sub-postmaster managing two offices, on a basis proportional to the work load of each, or even a Crown Office releasing staff to operate a part time village sub-office. This type of arrangement does occur, in fact, though it is usually restricted to offices where the level of business would otherwise justify a full time appointment but where there is no suitable person available to take up a full time post. Where the level of business is lower than this, the Post Office considers that the provision of part time services is too uneconomic. The overheads do not diminish proportionately but marginally, and for various reasons (including security) it is not often considered practicable to share overheads by, for instance, sharing premises.

As in many similar circumstances, one of the major decisions to be taken in these instances is on the relative weights to attach to the recognised social benefits on the one hand, including the factors relating to the travel costs and conveniences of users and, on the other hand, to the increased management costs. The rate of over four closures a week (and in many areas the parallel decline in public transport services) lends urgency to these questions, and to the need to monitor the characteristics of users and the effects of closure on them.

Health Services

Another important aspect of personal business is travel to health service facilities. Doctors and chemists have traditionally provided local services—the

NTS shows that 62 per cent of households live within ten minutes' walk of a chemist and for a surgery the proportion is 45 per cent. Dentists, too, are to be found in town centres, local high streets and residential areas, though there is no information available to quantify their accessibility. Some clinics are local to their users, often on a part time basis, with for example child care and family planning clinics making use of community halls or premises within housing estates—a PEP survey found that 46 per cent of housewives live within ten minutes' walk of a clinic.[13] Clinics and out-patient services attached to hospitals are, of course, less accessible: hospitals cater for a larger population, who also use the services less frequently. As a consequence the geographical catchment is wide and convenient access on foot becomes the exception rather than the rule. The NTS shows that only eight per cent of households live within ten minutes' walk of a hospital.

Each week there are about 9 visits made to doctors' surgeries for every 100 people, and a slightly greater number of prescriptions are dispensed (not all involving a separate journey). Women make more visits on their own behalf than men (additionally it is probable that mothers accompany children more often than do fathers). Although they have a high consultation rate, pensioners receive more visits at home, and so do not make an over proportionate number of journeys themselves.[14] Over half the pensioners in the PEP survey[15] walked when visiting their doctor and over 60 per cent walked to the chemist, as did the younger women surveyed—and if the young women had a chemist within ten minutes' walk, the proportion rose to almost 90 per cent. Of those using a clinic almost three quarters walked, the proportion again being higher if the clinic was within ten minutes' walk. Hospitals are visited less often than general practitioners, generating about three out-patient visits per 100 people each week, and motorised travel is more likely to be used, including specially provided transport.

As with post offices and schools, there is evidence of change over time in the geographical pattern of health service provision which implies reduced access to facilities. Like schools, the change is not only associated with the replacement of out-moded facilities or with shifts in the balance of population between different areas, but it is also associated with changes in the scale of facilities, and in the overall organisation of the service. In the context of local personal business travel, changes in the location of doctors' surgeries and chemist shops are of particular interest.

The grouping together of general practices and the development of health centres have both led to a reduction in the number of local surgeries. Between 1963 and 1975 the number of general practices in England fell by 13 per cent, from well over 10,000 to under 9,000—though the total number of doctors in them increased by about 9 per cent, with the average size of partnership increasing accordingly. In other words, over two practices a week disappeared during this time. The number of locations lost may have been even higher,

[13]M. Hillman et al, *Transport Realities and Planning Policy,* op.cit.
[14]OPCS Social Survey Division, *The General Household Survey 1976,* HMSO (1978).
[15]M. Hillman et al, *Transport Realities and Planning Policy,* op.cit.

because of the development of health centres in which a number of separate practices sometimes operate.

It is usually accepted that there are medical and economic benefits to be had from these two developments and that health centres particularly can foster the decentralisation of some hospital functions, thus making those functions more accessible to the users. But these factors should not obscure the less desirable effect of fewer surgeries generally resulting in reduced access to the general practitioner's services which are used by more people, and more frequently, than are the additional services that can be provided at a health centre. It is possible that reduced accessibility affects the use people are able to make of health services: one study has shown that individuals' consultation rates fell after a practice had moved to a health centre.[16]

It might be thought that the reduced number of doctors' practices would provide opportunties for more involvement by pharmacists in the treatment of minor ailments. However, this service, too, over time is to be found in fewer and fewer locations: the number of establishments fell by an average of nearly six a week between 1966 and 1976—that is, by over twenty per cent altogether.[17] At the same time the number of prescriptions dispensed has increased, indicating again that the average 'size' has increased while the number of outlets has decreased.[18]

To some extent the loss of chemists' shops is related to the developments in general practice: as the latter amalgamate or move to premises in health centres, so patients transfer their custom to pharmacists more conveniently sited in relation to their doctor's new location. Thus business declines in some establishments and increases in fewer others. In some cases the health centre itself contains a dispensary; moreover, items on general sale have increasingly become available on supermarkets. Thus turnover gradually declines in the local chemist until the establishment loses economic viability and closes. This may occur some years after a change in the location of doctors' practices and so it is not noted as being a direct result of such change in the surveys carried out annually by the Pharmaceutical Society.[19] Nevertheless, the Society acknowledges that the loss of economic viability, which is the reason most often cited for closure, is often precipitated by the movement of surgeries away from an area.

The Society also stresses the valuable social, community and medical function of the pharmacist (though there appears to be very little research into the consumer's use of and attitudes towards chemists or about the effects of chemists' closures) and is concerned at the continued loss of small local chemists. This concern was reflected in the relative increases in payments made to smaller pharmacies which were agreed by the Department of Health and Social Security early in 1978 after discussions with the Pharmaceutical Services

---

[16] *Trends in General Practice 1977*, Chapter 3, Patterns of Work, Essays by members of the Royal College of General Practitioners.

[17] Survey of Pharmacy Closures 1976, *The Pharmaceutical Journal*, July 2, 1977.

[18] Dispensing accounts for 60 per cent of pharmacists' business and other medical items for 10-12 per cent. (Source: The Pharmaceutical Society of Great Britain).

[19] Reported in *The Pharmaceutical Journal*.

Negotiating Committee (PSNC), but it is not yet possible to say what effect these increases have had in slowing down the decline in the number of small pharmacists. Part time pharmacies could provide a continuing service in areas where business had declined or has been siphoned off but there are very few of these and a difficulty exists in that the pharmacist would incur proportionately higher overhead costs and so perhaps require some form of subsidy.

Hospitals, too, have become fewer in number and larger in size over the years, implying larger catchment areas and an increase in the average distance that people need to travel to get to their nearest hospital, either as an in-patient, an out-patient or a visitor. The number of hospitals dropped by four per cent between 1970 and 1975,[20] including eight per cent for non-psychiatric hospitals,[21] with the decline being most extreme among the smallest units (with under 50 beds). The closure rate for non-psychiatric hospitals was equivalent to a loss of over three hospitals a month, including at least one a month of the smallest type traditionally often found in villages or small towns—and so within walking distance of a significant number of users.

General Trends

The information in the latter part of this chapter relates to only two types of personal business travel. Statistics on the provision of other facilities is restricted in scope or area (though other chapters document the decline associated with some other sectors of travel), and change is usually discussed in terms of operating costs and management systems. It is perhaps because the information is fragmented and gathered at different sources that the overall picture of change has not been defined and shifts in the patterns of land use, access and travel have not been fully documented or queried.

---

[20] In 1970 there were 2,808 hospitals in Great Britain; by 1975 this number had dropped to 2,684. Department of Health and Social Security *Health and Social Services Statistics 1976,* HMSO, (1977).

[21] In 1970, there were 2,397 non psychiatric hospitals; in 1975, the number had fallen to 2,204. Psychiatric hospitals, on the other hand have increased in numbers and reduced in size.

IX   Leisure Journeys

The NTS divides leisure journeys into five categories, the most commonly reported of these being *social activity*. This produced high journey rates per person both on foot and by other methods—over 10 journeys a day on foot and almost 30 by other methods for every 100 people. The next most common form of leisure travel ('day-trip/play') is also associated with about 10 walking journeys for every 100 people, but other travel methods add only a further eight journeys. The journey purpose is termed 'day trip/play' in the NTS, though in view of the high proportion of walking it is probably more appropriate to term it *recreation* for it includes going to parks and playgrounds and going for a walk, as well as outings for the day (which almost invariably involve motorised travel).[1]

The remaining three leisure categories account for fewer journeys and vary in their association with walking: the number of walk journeys per day are 3 per 100 people for *eating and drinking,* 3 per 100 for *entertainment* and 1 per 100 for *sport,* (representing about 40 per cent, 30 per cent and 20 per cent respectively of travel for each of these purposes).

Over one third of all the leisure journeys made on foot are less than half a mile in length, and one third are at least one mile. Journeys to public houses and other places for drinking or eating are shortest (half of these are under half a mile) and recreation journeys, where the walk itself may form part or all of the recreational activity, are longest (almost half being at least one mile long). Social visits also tend to involve a large proportion of short journeys no doubt reflecting a certain amount of neighbourhood activity. In the 1975/76 NTS it is likely that most of the neighbourly activity (i.e. calling on a neighbour) is excluded by virtue of the exclusion of the very shortest of journeys on foot (under 50 yards).

Indeed, the number of short journeys on foot (under half a mile) for all leisure activity appears to drop sharply between the two surveys. But the decline can by no means be wholly attributed to the conscious exclusion of the reporting of activity which involves just 'popping next door' or 'down the road'; in 1972/73 these journeys would have been included in the 'under a

---

[1]In this analysis the small number of mainly motorised holiday journeys have been included in the recreation category.

quarter of a mile' category, for which the journey rate fell from 10 per 100 in 1972/73 to 5 per 100 in 1975/76. However, the rate for journeys between a quarter and half mile also fell, from 8 per 100 in 1972/73 to 5 per 100 1975/76 and the rates for medium and longer walks also declined, though to a lesser extent. These figures imply a fairly substantial drop in the proportion of leisure activities reached on foot, in relation to places visited for eating or drinking as well as for social journeys. It appears that recreation journeys declined least, and retained a heavy emphasis on walking in both years, as Table IX.1 shows.

Table IX.1   Changes in leisure travel on foot, 1972/73 and 1975/76

	Per cent of journeys on foot		Walk journeys per person per day		Per cent of walks less than ½ mile	
	1972/73	1975/76	1972/73	1975/76	1972/73	1975/76
Social	32	27	0.13	0.10	57	43
Recreation	59	57	0.12	0.10	32	25
Eat/drink	49	42	0.06	0.03	43	36
Entertainment	33	29	0.04	0.03	64	51
Sport	30	23	0.01	0.01	40	38
All leisure activity	40	35	0.36	0.28	48	36

There are no strong differences in the pattern of walking journeys for leisure in different areas. There is somewhat less emphasis on walking in rural areas, especially for visiting places for eating or drinking, though the overall number of walk journeys is equivalent in both rural and metropolitan areas. In other urban areas, rather more walk journeys were reported, especially for social activity and, to a lesser degree, entertainment. Bearing in mind the variations in access to cars in the different areas the similarity of travel patterns is at first surprising, but it would appear that the greater range and choice of most leisure facilities in larger urban settlements, together with more extensive public transport networks found there, counter the effects of lower car ownership. Moreover, walking is somewhat reduced in metropolitan areas because they are relatively deficient in parks and open spaces—facilities which otherwise tend to be fairly local and associated with a high level of walking.

Personal Variation

At first sight, the variation in walking to a leisure activity reflects the car availability of different age groups. Pensioners report the highest proportion of journeys on foot and men of working age the lowest. Women, who are more likely to travel with their husbands on these journeys, walk somewhat less than their teenage and younger children. It might further be thought that reliance on walking would mean a reduced catchment or choice of opportunities and so, (on these optional journeys) less activity; less reliance on

Table IX.2 Leisure activity rates and the proportion of journeys on foot, according to journey purpose and age-sex group

Type of leisure activity	Children (3-11 years)		Teenagers (11-19 years)		Journeys on foot per person per day Men (21-64 years)		Women (21-59 years)		Men (65 years and over)		Women (60 years and over)	
	Number	*Per cent*	*Number*	*Per cent*	*Number*	*Per cent*	*Number*	*Per cent*	*Number*	*Per cent*	*Number*	*Per cent*
Social	0.33	33	0.46	35	0.41	17	0.42	25	0.31	26	0.30	37
Recreation	0.21	48	0.18	53	0.17	59	0.16	56	0.25	75	0.17	66
Eat/drink	0.01	41	0.06	42	0.17	46	0.06	29	0.08	60	0.02	49
Entertainment	0.09	46	0.15	32	0.08	19	0.09	24	0.06	39	0.06	28
Sport	0.06	18	0.13	34	0.07	13	0.03	19	0.03	16	—	—
All leisure activities	0.71	38	0.99	38	0.89	30	0.76	32	0.73*	47	0.55	46

*Walk journeys over 1 mile, in length represent 19 per cent of the total, compared with an average of 12 per cent for all age groups.

walking could lead to more activity. Such tendencies are apparent for some groups—women pensioners at one extreme and working age men at the other—but they are by no means general, for the relationships between the amount and pattern of walking, the extent of leisure activity and the level of personal mobility, are far from constant. Neither is the amount of walking merely a reflection of the different types of activity undertaken, though this does have some influence.

Table IX.2 indicates these varying relationships and influences for different people. Thus, the high proportion of walk journeys of men pensioners reflects a higher than average number of recreation journeys and also a high proportion of longer journeys on foot, for which other people might use motorised transport. Children, too, reported more recreational activity, but if on foot, theirs is undertaken nearer home. Women pensioners are more walk-oriented than most people (except for entertainment journeys) and appear to be more restricted in their choice of activity, reporting by far the lowest total number of leisure journeys. Teenagers do not follow any 'standard' patterns—they report somewhat higher than average walking but also a high level of activity especially for those activities not generally associated with walking, such as sport, entertainment and social activity. Hence they also report a larger number of longer journeys on foot, thus extending their leisure choices by walking further. The pattern for men of working age initially appears simply to reflect their mobility; they make relatively few journeys on foot and so have extended horizons and activity levels. But a closer look shows that this generally high level of leisure activity stems mainly from a large number of walk oriented eating/drinking journey purposes, no doubt including short trips to their 'local'! It is noticeable that except for this journey purpose, they report a similar level of leisure activity to that reported by women in the same age group, though the women are somewhat more walk-oriented.

When comparisons are made within rather than between each age and sex group, the influence of car ownership can be seen more strongly, and it also appears that the more reliance people place on walking, the less they go out. This is shown in Table IX.3 for all leisure, and for selected activities, for each age and sex group. The only exceptions to the general pattern are the increased levels of activity among men pensioners without cars in respect of their recreation, and eating and drinking activities, and for the latter purpose also among younger men without cars.

It might be thought that the variation according to household car ownership, in both the level of walking and the total amount of leisure activity, might result from a different balance of activity among different car ownership groups. For instance, it might be supposed that recreation is more significant for the leisure activity of non-car owners and entertainment for that of car owners. But further analysis shows that this is not the case, for car ownership only marginally affects the relative 'popularity', or 'take-up', of the different broad types of leisure activity. Indeed, some of the variation is contrary to what might be expected in view of people's mobility. Thus, while

Table IX.3 Relationship between the extent of walking and the level of leisure activity, by all travel methods

	Number of journeys by all methods*			Per cent of journeys on foot:		
	2 car house-hold	1 car house-hold	No car house-hold	2 car house-hold	1 car house-hold	No car house-hold
Children (Aged 3-10 years)						
All leisure	86	75	55	25	34	60
of which:						
social	38	38	23	23	29	54
recreation	25	23	15	45	39	67
sport	11	5	5	7	12	49
Teenagers (Aged 11-20 years)						
All leisure	120	102	82	25	40	47
of which:						
social	58	19	14	24	38	41
recreation	47	15	14	8	34	44
sport	39	14	10	21	35	42
Men (Aged 21-64 years)						
All leisure	97	93	76	20	24	55
of which:						
social	43	45	31	7	11	45
eat/drink	20	14	21	25	41	67
sport	10	7	4	4	10	36
Women (Aged 21-59 years)						
All leisure	81	81	64	18	29	47
of which:						
social	44	46	33	11	22	40
recreation	16	17	14	50	53	67
entertainment	10	8	7	3	21	42
Men (65 years and over)						
All leisure		80	69		30	61
of which:						
social		39	26		12	40
recreation		24	26		62	83
eat/drink		6	9		34	71
Women (60 years and over)						
All leisure		68	50		41	48
of which:						
social		31	29		26	42
recreation		26	13		67	66
entertainment		7	5		22	32

*Number of journeys per 100 people per day

sport (often involving a motorised journey) features more strongly among the leisure of car owners compared with non-car owners, the opposite is true of entertainment (also generally featuring motorised travel). Among women pensioners, social activity (again on the whole fairly motorised), assumes more importance for those without cars than for those with cars; recreational outings are less significant.

Of course, the activities in the NTS relate to broad categories of leisure, and within any category, there exists in practice a wide range of facility or location from local open space to country park, or from local bingo hall to grand opera house. It is probable—and data drom other sources supports the hypothesis[2] —that reliance on walking does not influence the broad type of activity but rather the particular type, including the characteristics or standard of facility visited. For example, local entertainment facilities are likely to be different in character and 'prestige' than those available, say, in town centres and so inaccessible to people travelling on foot. Moreover, in spite of the similarity in the broad profile of activity between population groups, what emerges strongly is that reliance on walking is associated with reduced levels of activity within each population group.

---

[2] See for example, the discussion on this subject in M. Hillman and A. Whalley, *Fair Play For All*, PEP Broadsheet 571, (1977).

X Conclusions

No one can deny that walking plays a significant role in personal travel, and the official national surveys used for this research have provided a measurement of just how significant this role is. Overall, more than one in three of all the journeys that people make are made, door-to-door, on foot. Every day people spend about an hour, on average, travelling to reach places they need or wish to visit, and one quarter of this time is spent on journeys wholly made on foot.[1] These journeys are generally short: almost three quarters of all walk journeys are under one mile in length, and well over one third are under half a mile. This means, therefore, that travel on foot for distances of less than half a mile is sufficient to meet a sixth of what is commonly considered to be total personal transport demand.

The 'average' extent of walking hides a wide range and a variety of patterns of pedestrian travel for different people and areas. A person's position within that range reflects, naturally, whether they have the personal use of a car, which in turn is influenced by factors such as their age, sex, income, and social group. These personal factors thus affect walking by determining whether a person can use a car, while the area in which they live, and the destination they seek, help to determine whether they then need to do so. To a lesser extent the same factors determine whether or not public transport (or another less common travel method) is used. The outcome of all these interactions is that walking accounts for about 8 in 10 of the journeys of pensioners without a car, but only 2 in 10 of the journeys of young men with a car; that a journey is three times as likely to be on foot if it is to a primary school rather than to a sports or entertainment facility; and that walking is almost twice as significant for travel in high density residential areas as for travel in low density areas.

Comparison of the findings of the two National Travel Surveys in 1972/73 and 1975/76 has shown that, as a means of reaching destinations, walking is in decline; people made about 5 per cent fewer of their journeys on foot in the later survey, representing a drop of about 12 per cent in the relative amount of walking recorded. On the other hand the average length of journey on foot has increased by over 10 per cent. The extent to which these facts are related to each other would seem to be an important policy question.

---

[1] In addition, the beginnings and ends of non-walk journeys are made on foot, sometimes involving fairly lengthy trips to bus stops, car parks or railway stations — though this aspect of walking has not been the subject of the research in this book.

In spite of the prominence of walking in daily travel, however, and the fact that the amount of walking varies in different situations, and is subject to policy influences, the review in the first chapter has strongly indicated that in both transport policy and practice, it has been overlooked or, at the least, has been inadequately recognised. A number of reasons could be suggested for this neglect; there is the conventional dominant concern in the transport field with the problems generated by past increases in traffic levels—and forecast future increases; there is the common view that longer journeys are more 'important' than shorter ones, a view which is reinforced by the fact that they are more likely to incur public expenditure and therefore to feature on the politicians' agenda. Likewise, it may be that walking is discounted because its use does not impose costs that then have to be met, for it generates few traffic problems and is therefore the antithesis of the type of technical challenges which transport planners have been trained to overcome. It may be that the dearth of published research on the subject—which it is hoped this study will have gone some way to remedy—partly explains it. And, of course, it may be pertinent, or perhaps impertinent, to suggest that decision makers in this field are less aware of the significance of walking because they tend to be less rather than more walk oriented in their own patterns of daily travel.

Whatever the reasons, however, the question to be asked is whether this neglect matters. This question can be answered by reference to issues which are set out below and which draw on the data and discussion in previous chapters. They are important firstly, because it is relevant to look more closely at the extent and significance of pedestrian travel for people in different walks of life. Secondly, it is relevant to examine how much walking appears to be changing and to assess the influences on and consequences of this for the transport 'consumer'. Thirdly, it is necessary to see whether walking is critical to the operation of the transport system as a whole and to the central concerns of transport policy.

There are grounds enough for concern about the official neglect of walking in the very fact that walking is not a minor travel method, and that it is not undertaken by only a minority of people. It is as if those involved with the formulation of transport policy and practice do not consider it to be a travel method, or that they consider its role in satisfying transport demand to be unimportant—whereas it has well-nigh universal relevance, irrespective of personal circumstance. Even in car owning households 28 per cent of journeys are made on foot; and even on the most highly motorised of journeys—to and from work—walking accounts for 19 per cent of the modal split, and is used by men, women and young people.

Nevertheless, as Chapter III in particular has shown, there are groups in society who rely far more heavily on walking than others, and it is necessary to be aware of whose interests are more affected by the lack of attention paid to walking. It is apparent from the earlier chapters that the neglect results in an under-representation in policy of the travel needs of those who could loosely be termed the more vulnerable groups in society, including most of the low paid and unskilled, most pensioners, and of course, most children—and women more than men. In determining how much concern there should be at this, account must be taken of two significant findings in this study. First, those who walk, or have to walk, or depend on walking (it is difficult to attribute motivation) make the fewest journeys. (It would clearly be presumptuous to assert that this is so because they have less need to make journeys). Second, their travel patterns are more walk oriented not only because of their low level of access to a car but also because the public transport system does not provide a fully satisfactory alternative—as indicated by their use of walking being much higher than their use of public transport, and their use of public transport being far lower than other people's use of cars. They are, therefore, being unfairly treated, in that relatively little consideration is paid to the character and convenience of their major transport method.

Furthermore, it is not only the character and convenience of walking that needs mention in this respect, for travel methods, though important in themselves, are used as a means of achieving something else. They provide access to other people and places, and they define the catchment of opportunities open to their users. Walking effectively defines a limited catchment of opportunities for those people who rely on it as their 'staple diet' for transport, and few of them are prepared to, or can, spend much time in walking. This limitation is likely to be overlooked by the neglect of walking. The neglect—and its converse the concentration on motorised travel—can also result in the opportunities becoming further restricted by the implementation of measures aimed at increasing the efficiency of motorised travel, or aimed at economising or rationalising the provision of retailing, education, leisure facilities and so on. In this respect, decisions in the field of planning as well as of transport should equally be made with an awareness of their implications for walking. Associated with these issues of equity, account must be taken of the data in Chapters II and III which show that pedestrians are at greater risk of being harmed or killed in road accidents than are car or bus users—a risk to which what we have called the vulnerable groups are more exposed because of their reliance on walking. Chapter II has shown that each year over 20,000 people are killed or seriously injured when walking, a figure which has changed little in the last few years. There were in fact somewhat fewer of these accidents in 1976 than in 1973, but the drop did not match the drop in the number of walk journeys perhaps partly because the walk journeys became longer. Moreover, the number of car journeys did not decline.

The change in the amount of walking over time is itself an issue worthy of more attention from those concerned with transport policy and practice, if only because walking has so far satisfied such a significant amount of daily travel. It is difficult to see how appropriate decisions can be taken without some assessment of whether the decline in walking is good or bad for those contributing to it, and of whether it represents journeys foregone or journeys transferred to other methods. The research in this book has indicated that the change is not a simple transfer but a kaleidoscopic change of modes, destinations and activity levels. Moreover, there is a need to ascertain whether a transfer to motorised travel represents increased mobility or reduced accessibility (which then necessitates motor travel). Evidence cited from sources other than the NTS does in fact suggest the change in travel is at least partly explained by changes in access arising from planning and rationalising changes previously mentioned.

Much of the change in walking is, however, a reflection of changing mobility—that is, the increasing number of people with access to a car. The relevance of this to policy analysis is that the change in walking is sometimes the affected element but sometimes the causal element in this relationship: analysis and projections about car ownership and use, therefore, need to include consideration of the potential for walking. Earlier chapters have shown that areal characteristics are influential on walking which varies both with proximity—that is, whether the destination to be reached is easily accessible on foot—and with residential density. Car ownership is also affected because access, or rather the lack of it, can create situations requiring frequent car travel and so, in practice, car ownership particularly when, as is often the case, lack of access is combined with the absence of good public transport. It is further possible, though less obvious, that access is in turn influenced by car ownership: car owners may use their cars to exercise choice and visit facilities which are larger or better or more suited to their needs and preferences than those provided locally. Such action could then have the effect of reducing the viability of, or perceived demand for, locally accessible facilities and services, and this could then bring about their closure in spite of some people's reliance on them.

In fact, this situation does not always arise, as analysis in earlier chapters indicates that short distances sometimes suffice to fulfil the travel needs or preferences of people with cars, as well as the needs of people without cars. Thus, not only does car and multi-car ownership drop markedly in areas of high density which tend to have more facilities accessible locally, but so does car use among those with a car. Indeed, the gap between car owners and non-car owners, in the extent of their walking, gradually and continually diminishes as population density increases.

The issues mentioned so far are concerned with the travel of individuals and could be said to be issues of 'consumer' interest to be taken into account when viewing the neglect of walking and the lack of policy on pedestrian travel. Other issues relate to wider interests or are of more direct concern to those responsible for making transport policy and putting it into practice.

The first of these issues relates to the overall balance of travel, a balance traditionally seen as one between the motorised elements of travel (including railways), capable of manipulation through policy on such travel. But it should be recognised that walking also plays a significant role within this balance, even, for instance, as regards the travel of people with cars, or on the journey to work. Transfers to or from walking can alter the relative balance of other methods of travel if the transfers are disproportionately spread among those other methods. Data in earlier chapters have shown that this does happen, and that the decline in walking increases the amount of car travel relative to that of public transport. Controlling the car and public transport balance through transport and planning measures could thus prove abortive if those measures—or other events—also influence the level of pedestrian travel.

The fact that this issue has not been explicitly recognised is all the more serious when the generalised economic and time costs of the transfer from walking are high. For example, the transfer from walking can be seen to be aggravating the rush hour problem in view of the inevitably limited capacity of the road network and the consequent need to oblige commuters to travel by public transport. This can render the service more costly to operate as more buses and trains and crews are needed at peak travelling times but are then under-utilised at other times of the day.

Of even wider concern is the fact that the transfer from walking is high in terms of energy costs. It was noted earlier that walking at present satisfies over one third of the country's travel demands; what needs stressing here is that this is achieved with no petrol consumption. For instance, the growth of low density residential developments, and the segregation of land uses has meant that more and more people are becoming less walk-oriented in their patterns of daily travel. To pay little attention to these trends is irresponsible, given the prospect of a future in which the costs of motor fuel are likely to escalate, and in which its uninterrupted availability is by no means assured. In this respect, the contribution that transport policy can make to the national aims of energy conservation and the sensible use of resources needs to be borne in mind; these national aims are not advanced by the process of transfer from walking to motorised patterns of travel. One example of the effect of this transfer can be seen in the taking of a young child by car to and from a school which is, say, just one mile away, for this then requires four miles' worth of petrol a day — double this, if the child returns home for lunch. Data in Chapter V have indicated that by 1975/76 about one in seven primary school children were travelling to school by car over varied distances, and that this had increased over time inline with the decline in, and lengthening of, walk journeys.

Finally, the neglect of pedestrian travel is disturbing in so far as it is apparent that walking has other beneficial characteristics which are not considered in decisions about transport and planning policy and in evaluations about transport change. These include the fact that is it a quiet and non-polluting form of transport, a cheap way of getting around, that it represents a minor form of exercise conducive to good health and, because it is associated with local activity, is likely to engender conviviality and neighbourliness within the community.

On all these grounds it would appear that to neglect walking is to neglect a major and basic component of the transport system; that there is a need for policy to assesss the role that walking plays — and could further play — in meeting transport demand; and that walking should be incorporated into the panoply of transport modes to which transport policy is directed and which are used in the development of planning policy.

It is likely that the inclusion of the consideration of walking as a method of travel in both transport and planning policy would provide a new perspective for policy. But it would not also require a change in the framework, for the potential exists within the present framework for the inclusion of walking into transport policy and for the development of a policy on walking itself. For instance, such existing basic aims and issues of transport policy as are set out in the 1977 White Paper on Transport Policy, do not preclude consideration of pedestrian travel any more than they preclude consideration of travel by car, or bus, or train. These aims and issues relate to meeting the travel needs of the population and providing access to opportunities, to the cost-effectiveness of different methods of travel, to the energy requirements of alternative means of transport or planning systems, to the environmental consequences of travel, and to the need for safety in travel.

These issues also feature in development plans, which thereby also have the scope for including consideration of walking and the assessment of patterns of development which engender greater or lesser amounts of pedestrian travel. This is true for statutory structure plans as well as, more obviously, for local plans. Walking is a strategic issue in the travel of most people and is of structural importance both to the operation of the transport system and to the choices available in land use and locational planning.

If policy is to be based on these aims and issues and if it is also to take proper account of pedestrian travel then it needs to examine the consequences of society becoming less walk oriented — which seems to be the current trend. To this end it is necessary, for instance, to incorporate walking into the tests of financial performance of alternative systems of transport, in order to ascertain whether there are costs that could be avoided by maintaining or even increasing the amount of travel demand currently met on foot. Indeed, it is worthwhile noting the contention of the 1977 White Paper that 'each mode of transport must be judged on the same criteria and encouraged to do what it can do best in terms of both economic and social costs'. Clearly, in judging pedestrian travel it is necessary to consider that it meets travel demand without incurring the economic and social costs known to be associated with motorised travel — costly road construction and maintenance, noise, air pollution, energy consumption and so on. However, there is scope for research to make a considerable contribution to policy here by establishing more precisely than is currently known the private and public advantages and disadvantages — social, environmental, energy, as well as financial — of the transfer from walking to motorised forms of travel, and vice-versa, to get to work, school, shops, leisure facilities and so on. Research could also establish the means of encouraging or discouraging such transfers.

Such an approach requires an examination of the circumstances within which some people have the ability to lead lives without as much recourse to motor travel, that is having to make few journeys by motorised means. At present the needs of people travelling by motorised means are given greater emphasis in that the more they travel the greater are the benefits accruing to them of transport investment. Associated with the assessment of transport systems, therefore, is the need to monitor and evaluate planning or locational changes associated with changes in the balance of travel.

In parallel with this is the need to consider the accessibility characteristics of different areas, facilities and zoning policies from the point of view of the opportunity afforded to people with different levels of mobility and also from the point of view of the traffic they generate. In the latter instance, such measures could additionally be of use in analysing future energy requirements and in calculating where there is potential for the probable future constraints on the energy available for transport.

Recognition of the requirements of pedestrians themselves is a further consequence of a policy which takes proper account of pedestrian travel. There is a need to consider the interests of pedestrians, having regard to access, convenience and safety. This would be aided through the establishment of divisions within central and local government whose concern it would be to look after these interests, identifying where and how they could be served. The medium through which they would operate would be statutory and advisory instruments of policy — the development plans, the TPPs, the Circulars, the Design Bulletins and Manuals and so on.

As regards access, planners need to bear in mind how conducive proximity is to walking and how the ability to do without a car is linked with good access — on foot. They need, too, to be aware of who is affected by changes in the local availability of facilities and to know what effects planning activity is having on this and on the aim of providing opportunities for the population at large. In this respect it would be advantageous for future National Travel Surveys to widen the present coverage of accessibility — limited as it is at present to establishing distances to respondents' nearest outlets for some personal business activity — to aid in establishing broad guidelines on access.

Moreover, where land use planners themselves are not responsible for changes in the access of facilities, such information would be of use to those who are responsible, especially if presented together with the planners' analysis of the implications for the public's travel to, and use of, the particular type of facility concerned — whether health services or sports provision. All too often emphasis is placed on the benefits to future users of providing large scale, well-equipped, modern facilities and the economies of scale which can be achieved. But attention is not paid to the corollary — the effects on their users of the withdrawal of smaller, locally available facilities. Indeed, such provision may be false economy in some instances if the lack of local facilities then requires an increase in domiciliary services or special transport to the elderly who are among those most reliant on walking.

The convenience aspects of walking — the easy movement on foot with the minimum of changes in level, of exposure to the weather and of delay in crossing roads — fall within the purview of the transport planner. Transport research is also needed to determine the tolerance of pedestrians to these factors in order to show what standards are appropriate for kerb heights, pavement widths and traffic or pedestrian lights phases, and to determine the benefits of such design features as seating or arcades or other forms of cover on the pedestrian network. Such seemingly minor aspects of convenience in travel have, after all, featured in respect of research into vehicular travel and in the practices associated with public transport operation, traffic management and, for example, parking provision.

Pedestrians' safety and convenience will be improved when the clause in the 1974 Road Traffic Act making pavement parking illegal becomes mandatory in 1980. The problem of enforcing the law on this is likely to be simple, provided the penalty is severe — a stiff fine with perhaps the addtional inconvenience of a trip to the police pound to recover the vehicle could well ensure observance of the law in the future. Convenience could be further enhanced by keeping pavements clean and clear of other obstructions, such as street furniture which are a nuisance for people with prams or pushchairs and young children, and an obvious hazard for blind and partially sighted people.

At a more strategic level, what is needed from the pedestrian's viewpoint is a total network, preferably uninterrupted at road intersections by kerbs, guardrails and large numbers of fast-moving vehicles. The pedestrian precincts established in the central areas of some towns and cities in Britain are a start. But they have limited applicability and, in effect, they are islands of safety isolated from the rest of town by rivers of traffic, thus, in practice, largely accessible only by motorised means. The concept of traffic free rooms and motorised corridors unfortunately disregards the need for convenient pedestrian movement between the rooms. Consideration thus needs to be given to what are the reasonable time and distance limits for pedestrians, as well as other road users, to be delayed or detoured. And, insofar as pedestrians are part of the transport system, thought needs to be directed towards the need to provide a more equal partnership between pedestrians and motor traffic at intersections. This could be done by, for example, the use of traffic light phasing or pedestrian crossing facilities, the extension of the 'no-go' areas at yellow box junctions, or changes in the road levels and textures at intersections to indicate that a stretch of road is joint space.

The final major requirement of the pedestrian is to be able to travel without undue risk of injury and yet, as noted in Chapter II, each year over 20,000 people are killed or seriously injured when walking. The need for improvement in safety standards and the enforcement of existing traffic laws seems imperative, and could well require concerted action on several fronts. Politicians, the media and the general public, as well as traffic managers, have obvious roles to play.

It is disturbing that so many people have to pay such a high price for their own or another's momentary lapse of concentration when many preventive and proven measures of accident prevention are available — such as reducing traffic speeds, providing pedestrian crossing facilities and clamping down on drunken driving — and drunken pedestrians. Research is still needed however, to reveal what realistic limits can be instituted to reduce the risk to pedestrians when crossing roads, what costs and benefits are associated with higher and lower speeds, and what are the speeds at which it is safe enough for pedestrians and vehicles to share common ground.

One problem in this respect is public acceptability. In the past, those opposed to lower speeds have been able to argue with some justice that, however inviting the prospect, they could not work, because of problems of compliance by the motoring public. Indeed, it has been the view of the police that they would not wish to see the introduction of laws which they do not have the manpower to enforce. (It is widely acknowledged that only a very small proportion of motorists who exceed the speed limit are prosecuted.) But since the 1974 Road Traffic Act, local authorities have been allowed to install road humps on a temporary basis on public roads. In view of the success of the few experiments that have been tested, the government could legislate to enable local authorities to install them permanently and to provide a network of them on appropriate roads if they so wish. One could speculate then that were only one authority to take such action on the roads under its control, and to provide pedestrian crossings wherever the current criteria for their installation are met, it could establish an enviable reputation by justifiably being able to claim that, after say twelve months operation, so many more of its citizens were alive and well as a direct result. At the same time, this action could encourage other authorities to follow suit for fear of accusation that they were accessories before the fact in relation to their own citizens' deaths and injuries in road accidents. Indeed, it would be a dare-devil politician who, in the circumstances, would reverse this decision on the grounds that the travel time lost due to the lower speed limit was worth more than the saving of life and limb and the avoidance of so much grief.

In conclusion, for the proper integration of walking into policy some of the issues raised in this chapter must be explored. Are people in fact better off or worse off if they make increasingly more of their journeys by motorised means rather than on foot, or if their daily travel needs are met over increasing distances? Or would the community benefit from people being encouraged to adopt life styles which become more walk oriented? Indeed, how can transport and planning policy be appropriately determined without establishing the advantages and disadvantages both to the individual and to the community of all the major methods of travel as well as of changes in the balance of people's patterns of travel — including walking.

Appendix A

Note on the National Travel Survey and Definition of Terms Used

1. The National Travel Survey (NTS) 1972/73 was carried out by a Market Research Agency for the Department of the Environment (DoE), using a nationwide sample, from April 1972 to March 1973 inclusive. The NTS 1975/76 was carried out for the Department of Transport (DTp), from July 1975 to June 1976 inclusive.

2. The surveys comprised household and individual questionnaires, and included a week-long travel diary for each individual down to, and including, those aged three years. Walk journeys of at least one mile were included throughout the whole week but walk journeys of under a mile were included on only one day of the survey — the final day, which fell on a different day of the week for different people. This report can thus make use of only one day's travel from the travel diary.[1]
The published DoE/DTp documents[2] on the NTS use data from the whole diary and so need to be viewed with caution because of the bias arising from the incomplete records of the first six days of the survey.

3. The data used in this report cover, for the 1972/73 survey, over 7 thousand households, over 20 thousand individuals and over 48 thousand journeys; and for the 1975/76 survey, over 15 thousand households, over 33 thousand individuals and over 71 thousand journeys.

4. The two surveys were based on the same aims and scope, but there are differences in their coverage, definitions used and in some of the detailed content. Comparison is thus more difficult than would appear at first sight. Moreover, the two sets of data cannot be processed in an identical way (by outside users such as Policy Studies Institute) because of restrictions in the computer programming, especially in respect of the 1972/73 survey. A substantial amount of additional manual processing was therefore needed in order to produce the type of information presented in this report.

5. The surveys were not based on a cohort sample; indeed, the later survey included almost twice as many respondents as the former. The profile of

---

[1] See para 6 below.
[2] Department of the Environment, *National Travel Survey 1972/73, Cross-sectional analysis of passenger travel in Great Britain,* HMSO, (1975); Department of the Environment, *National Travel Survey, Number of journeys per week by different types of households, individuals and vehicles,* HMSO, (1976); *National Travel Survey 1972/73, a comparison of 1965 and 1972/73 surveys* — Social Survey Division, Office of Population Censuses and Surveys, 1976.

respondents also varied somewhat, as did the areas in which they lived. (See Appendix B)

6. One difference between the surveys which is of especial relevance for this report relates to the coverage of walk journeys. Both surveys, as noted above, excluded walks of under one mile in the first six days of the travel diaries, but the 1975/76 survey also excluded the very shortest walks of less than 50 yards, in the diaries' final day. Although the number of journeys involved is no doubt small, it could nevertheless represent an important element of the travel of certain groups or areas, or for certain journey purposes. Numerically, moreover, these journeys could be as significant as *all* train travel. Under 500 rail journeys (of any distance) were reported on the final day of the survey and almost 5,500 walk journeys of under a quarter mile were recorded on the same day representing an average rate of over 700 walk journeys per additional 50 yards travel. (This calculation is based on the assumption that walks of under a quarter mile are evenly distributed according to distance).

7. Another variation relates to the number of journeys for which the travel method is unknown. The method assigned to a journey is that which is used for the longest part of the journey. For example if a *journey* consists of the following three *stages* — a walk of 100 yards to a bus stop, a bus ride of five miles and then another walk of half a mile — it will be recorded as a bus journey. Where the distances for the separate parts of the journey are not known the journey cannot be assigned to any method. This situation occurred on 10 per cent of (final day) journeys in the 1975/76 survey but only on one per cent of journeys in the 1972/73 survey. It has not been possible to assign these journeys with total confidence, and neither is the DTp able to do so, but what has been ascertained is that they consisted of more than one stage, and that about half the stages were on foot. In this study, and after further analysis, it has been concluded that it is reasonable to assign them to motorised travel, probably in the ratio equivalent to that reported for the individual stages: 60 per cent are probably car journeys and 40 per cent public transport. Officials at the DTp working on the NTS concur with this view.

8. There are other differences between the surveys, in definition and in the detailed content and administration of the questionnaire which, it is understood, will be the subject of a future comparative report from the DTp.

Definitions

9. *Journey:* implies one-way travel from origin to destination, and not a 'round trip'. A journey may consist of a number of *stages,* reflecting a change of travel method or interchange between, say, two buses.

10. *Journey rate:* calculated in this report as the number of journeys made on one day by one (or 100 or 1000) individual(s). Rates are calculated on the basis of individual respondents with full response in their record books; the rates therefore, exclude individuals, and their journeys, whose record books were known to have some journeys missing.

11. *Purpose:* the purpose allocated to each journey is that of the activity undertaken at the destination, unless the destination is 'home', in which case the purpose allocated is that of the origin.

12. *Multi-purpose journey:* this term is used in this report for journeys which neither begin nor end at home: for example, a journey from work to shops, or from the cinema to a public house. The purpose allocated to the journey remains that of the destination, i.e. shopping and eating/drinking in the above examples.

13. *Car ownership:* this term is used in this report to denote ownership of a '3-4 wheeled vehicle' as defined in the NTS. This includes ownership of a van, whereas the NTS definition of car ownership is strictly limited to cars.

14. *Non-licence holder* in this report includes people holding a provisional driving licence.

15. *Teenagers:* in this report relates to young people aged 11-20 inclusive except where stated otherwise. It is not possible to identify individual year groups in the NTS and analysis shows that the 16-20 year group, even though covering the age at which a driving licence can first be obtained, has more in common with 11-15 year-olds than with 21-29 year-olds.

16. *SEG:* this report uses the General Household Survey definitions of socio-economic group, which in turn stem from the Registrar General's classification of occupations as used in the NTS. The groupings are as follows:

SEG		Occupation reference no.
1	Professional	3,4
2	Employers and managers	1,2,13
3	Intermediate and junior non-manual	5,6
4	Skilled manual and own account non-professional	8,9,12,14
5	Semi-skilled manual and personal service	7,10,15
6	Unskilled manual	11

SEG groups 1, 2 and 3 are white-collar; 4, 5 and 6 are blue-collar.

17. *Density:* the NTS population densities are measured on a ward basis relating to population per hectare and classified as follows:

(low)	1—up to 1.25	people per hectare
	2—1.25 to 2.5	,, ,,
	3—2.5 to 6	,, ,,
	4—6 to 12	,, ,,
	5—12 to 18	,, ,,
	6—18 to 25	,, ,,
	7—25 to 37	,, ,,
	8—37 to 50	,, ,,
	9—50 to 75	,, ,,
(high)	10—75 and over	,, ,,

18. *Settlement size:* this relates to de facto urban areas specified by the Regional Plans Directorate of the Department of the Environment.

19. *Income:* relates to gross household income in 1975/76 or 1972/73 as appropriate.
In Table VI.3: high income = £4,000 and over per year
low income = under £4,000 per year.

Appendix B

Profile of Respondents in National Travel Survey 1972/73 and 1975/76

1. As a background to a comparison of the patterns of journeys made in the National Travel Surveys of 1972/73 and 1975/76, it is necessary to establish in what respects the samples of respondents in the two surveys differ in their personal and household characteristics. It is also relevant to compare the areal characteristics of the two samples where possible.

Age and sex

2. Table B.1 shows that, with the exception of a small increase in the proportion of young teenagers and a small decrease in the proportion of children of primary school age in the later survey, the two samples compare well in each of the three age groups below the age of 16. Similarly, when broken down by age and sex, the adult groups are closely matched, although in the later survey the proportion of men and women over the age of retirement is somewhat higher, being balanced by the inclusion of slightly fewer younger adults.

Table B.1   Respondents by age group and sex

	NTS 1972/73	NTS 1975/76
	Per cent	
Age of children:		
3—4 years	3.4	3.2
5—10 years	11.6	10.9
11—15 years	8.2	8.9
Age of men:		
16—20 years	3.2	3.0
21—29 years	5.8	5.6
30—59 years	18.6	18.1
60—64 years	2.7	2.7
65 years and over	5.4	6.0
Age of women:		
16—20 years	3.2	3.3
21—29 years	6.4	6.4
30—59 years	19.9	19.4
60 years and over	11.3	12.1
All groups	100	100
Sample size (number)	16,792	27,583

SEG of Head of Household and Household Status of Respondent

3. Comparison of the SEG of the heads of households of respondents in the two surveys can be seen in Table B.2. This shows that in the later survey the share of the white collar groups is slightly higher. The distribution of the respondents' household status is identical in the two surveys, with 37 per cent being heads of households, 27 per cent wives of the heads, 13 per cent other adults and 23 per cent children.

Table B.2   Respondents by SEG of head of household

Socio-economic groups	NTS 1972/73	NTS 1975/76
	Per cent	
1	5	6
2	15	16
3	18	18
4	40	39
5	17	15
6	4	5
Other groups	1	2
All groups	100	100

Type of Area

4. Table B.3 shows that the type of area in which the respondents lived varied quite markedly. In the later survey, there was an appreciably smaller proportion from the conurbations and medium-sized towns (with populations of 25-100,000), but a much higher representation from rural areas and small settlements. Indeed, the proportions from areas with less than 3,000 people was doubled in the later survey.

Planning Region

5. Analysis of respondents to the two surveys according to the planning region in which they lived reveals less difference: Table B.4 shows that the most marked differences are the decline in the later survey in the proportion of respondents from Scotland and the Yorkshire and Humberside region, and an increase of those from Wales and the South West.

Household Car Ownership and Licence Holding

6. As Table B.5 shows, the proportions of households either with one or with two or more cars were higher in the later survey. The table also shows that, particularly when analysed by household income, multi-car ownership appears to have increased at a faster rate than single car ownership. However, the increases are not to the degree that might be expected in view of the much higher rural and slightly higher white collar representation in the later survey, both of these factors being associated with high household car ownership.

Table B.3   Respondents by types of area

	NTS 1972/73	NTS 1975/76
Metropolitan areas	*Per cent*	
London	14.3	11.2
Birmingham	4.7	4.3
Manchester	4.1	4.9
Glasgow	4.5	1.7
Liverpool	2.1	1.4
Other settlements (population size in 000's)		
250—1,000	14.2	12.9
100—250	11.4	13.4
50—100	10.0	7.1
25—50	11.2	8.6
3—25	15.4	18.3
Under 3	8.2	16.3
All settlements	100	100

Table B.4   Respondents by planning region

Planning region	NTS 1972/73	NTS 1975/76
	Per cent	
Scotland	10.9	8.5
North	6.6	5.8
Yorkshire and Humberside	10.7	9.2
North West	13.4	12.6
Wales	4.0	5.6
West Midlands	9.4	9.6
East Midlands	6.4	7.5
East Anglia	3.1	3.7
Greater London	9.7	10.1
South East (excluding Greater London)	18.6	18.6
South West	7.2	8.6
All regions	100	100

Table B.5 Respondents' household car ownership by household income

| | Cars in household: | | |
	Two or more	One	None
	Per cent		
NTS 1972/73	13	47	40
NTS 1975/76	15	48	37
Household income:			
Lowest quartile			
NTS 1972/73	1	22	76
NTS 1975/76	2	26	72
Highest quartile			
NTS 1972/73	31	54	15
NTS 1975/76	36	52	13

Appendix C

Car Ownership Correlates

Table C.1 Household car ownership and licence holding, by sex and age group of respondents, 1975/76

Household with:	Two or more cars		One car		No car		All households	
Respondent has:	Licence	No licence	Licence	No licence	Licence	No licence	Licence	No licence
Pensioners:			*Per cent*					
Men 65 and over	3	1	29	7	8	52	40	60
Women 60 and over	2	2	7	20	1	68	10	90
All	2	2	14	15	3	63	20	80
Men aged:								
21-29	19	1	48	4	10	17	77	23
30-59	19	—	54	3	7	17	80	20
60-64	12	1	46	3	6	32	64	36
All	18	—	52	3	8	18	78	22
Women aged:								
21-29	11	2	27	28	4	27	42	58
30-59	14	4	22	31	2	27	38	62
All	13	4	23	31	2	27	38	62
Children and teenagers:								
3-10	n.a.	16	n.a.	54	n.a.	30	n.a.	100
11-15	n.a.	17	n.a.	52	n.a.	30	n.a.	100
16-20	11	12	8	37	2	29	21	78
All	18		52		31		100	

Table C.2 Household car ownership by household income and socio-economic group of head of household 1975/76

	Two or more car household	One car household	No car household
Household income		*Per cent*	
£10,000 p.a. or over	72	24	5
£9,900—£7,500 p.a.	52	42	6
£7,499—£5,000 p.a.	26	58	16
£4,999—£3,000 p.a.	13	72	27
£2,999—£1,500 p.a.	5	45	51
Under £1,500 p.a.	1	15	84
SEG of head of household			
1	39	57	5
2	34	54	11
3	12	56	32
4	10	54	36
5	6	40	54
6	4	23	73

Reports already published

The POLICY STUDIES INSTITUTE (PSI) is a British independent policy research organisation concerned with issues relevant to economic and social policies and the working of political institutions.

PSI was formed in April 1978 through the merger of Political and Economic Planning (PEP), founded in 1931, and the Centre for Studies in Social Policy (CSSP), founded in 1972. It continues the tradition of both organisations to establish the facts by impartial empirical research and to relate the findings to practical policy making. The scope of the Institute's work has been extended by the recent establishment of a European Centre for Political Studies. PSI's work is financed by grants for specific studies made by trusts, foundations and public bodies, with substantial support from donations by industry and commerce, and by annual subscriptions.

The results of the studies are disseminated widely by means of frequent publications, articles and seminars.

1-2 Castle Lane, London SW1E 6DR
Telephone: 01-828 7055

How to obtain PSI publications

PSI publications may be obtained from booksellers or direct from PSI. Postage and packing will be additional to the cost of the publication if it is sent by post.

A list of recent publications and subscription details will be sent on request to PSI at 1-2 Castle Lane, London SW1E 6DR.